BURN YOUR MORTGAGE

OWN PROPERTY DEBT- FREE

REAL ESTATE

LEGACY BUILDER

FIRST HOME PURCHASED AT 19

PATRICK DEWAYNE HALL SR.

PHall Publishing and Entertainment LLC
3945 Richard Arrington Jr Blvd
Birmingham, Alabama 35234
Email: elevation087@gmail.com

Social Media:

Facebook: @ElevatedPat
Instagram: @ElevatedPat
TikTok: @ElevatedPat
YouTube: @ElevatedPat
Twitter/X: @ElevatedPat

Printed in the United States of America

First Edition: 2025

Cover design and interior layout by PHall Publishing and Entertainment LLC

For rights, permissions, media requests, or speaking engagements, contact the publisher directly.

DEDICATION

To you—the reader bold enough to invest in elevation.

This book is dedicated to your vision, your vibration, and your refusal to settle for less than you deserve. You didn't just buy a book… you made a declaration: to rise, to own, and to transform your mindset and your legacy.

May each chapter be a key that unlocks not only property—but purpose.

Welcome to your next level.

ACKNOWLEDGMENTS

To every block that taught me before I ever drafted a sentence, thank you.

To the elders whose memory corrected my understanding of value, who whispered legacy beneath blue tarps and behind boarded doors: your rhythm lives here.

To the families who refused bad appraisals, wrote their own market logic, and called out theft masked as professionalism, this book owes you everything.

To my community, who did not let me write abstract theory, but demanded truth tied to mortgages, repair invoices, and porch rituals: you refined every chapter.

To the young builders who don't just flip properties but flip narratives, keep teaching backwards systems how rhythm sounds when it moves right.

To my spiritual circle, whose prayers held the foundation steady even when language failed: this work is stitched with your breath.

To every reader with ashes in their hand and blueprints in their heart, you are the reason legacy survives.

And to the home that changed me: I still see you. I still serve you. I still write for the walls that held me.

Thank you.

TABLE OF CONTENTS

INTRODUCTION

This book isn't here to impress the industry, it's here to unchain you from it.

If you've picked up this book, you're not just looking to buy real estate, you're looking to elevate. To step into ownership without shackles. To rewrite the rules of what freedom looks like for you and your family.

Let me tell you this: You were never meant to chase someone else's version of success. You were never meant to spend your life working in someone's real estate office just to be close to property wealth, while watching others climb the ladder. You are meant to own, not observe. You are meant to walk into rooms as the buyer, not beg for approval from brokers, banks, or bosses.

This is not a textbook. It's a liberation manual.

We've been sold lies dressed as opportunities. They told us to go to real estate school so we could "get ahead" but most of us got stuck. Working in firms that teach us just enough to serve others, but never enough to own for ourselves. We were never taught how to appraise value through the lens of protecting our families, not just flipping houses for profit.

Let's be clear: You don't need a degree to gain real estate knowledge. You need hunger. You need access to information, books like this, and the willingness to open your mind wide enough to transform your life.

This book will teach you what the schools won't. It will show you how to buy property with no money down. But more importantly, it will show you how to think. How to recognize when you're being sold a dream wrapped in danger. How to stop mistaking "cute" homes for safe ones. Because let's be real: fresh paint and granite countertops do not erase crime. They don't heal neighborhoods. And they damn sure don't guarantee value.

We must elevate.

We must stop being fooled.

Who made the appraiser the boss of the bag?

Who decided what something costs... and why do we keep believing it?

Agents and appraisers often slap six-figure price tags on homes in broken communities. Why? Because their commission rides on it. The higher the value they assign, the bigger the cut they take. They don't care if the school down the street is failing. They don't care if the playground is overgrown with weeds or if the house across the street has shattered windows and a history of eviction notices. They care about their percentage.

But here's the truth: your life is worth more than a property in a neighborhood that puts it at risk.

Don't fall for the illusion. A home is not just walls and flooring, it's where your children sleep, where you recover your peace, where you build legacy. And if the community around it is riddled with violence, drugs, institutional neglect, and systemic disrepair, then the true value of that home is below zero.

This book is going to teach you how to recognize those traps.

It's going to show you how to negotiate differently. How to ask questions they're not used to hearing. How to read between the lines of every listing, walk through every rehab with clear eyes, and say, "No, that doesn't work for me."

And if you've ever been denied a loan, ignored by realtors, or told your credit score wasn't good enough, this book is your answer. Because we're not relying on traditional financing here. We're talking seller financing. Lease options. Subject-to deals. Creative strategies that help you get in without selling your soul to a lender who doesn't even want to see your zip code.

We are done chasing acceptance.

We are done being impressed by shiny facades and inflated price tags.

We're stepping into real ownership.

I won't teach you how to buy a mansion. I'm here to teach you how to buy a movement, a property that builds power, not just equity. One that serves your family, shields your future, and makes you the foundation of something greater.

This isn't just about homes. It's about healing.

It's about walking into neglected communities and saying, "We deserve better."

It's about creating a system of value that includes your life, your children's safety, and your right to build wealth on your terms.

There are homes for sale right now in communities where no child can play outside without fear. No credit union lends. No hospital heals. But still—the price tag says

$150,000. Why? Because someone cleaned it up just enough to make it look valuable. That's manipulation. And you won't fall for it anymore.

You are the appraiser now.

You determine the worth, not based on market hype, but based on truth, safety, community function, and vision.

This book will walk you through every chapter of that process. From how to understand the language of real estate to how to talk to sellers and structure deals. From how to rehab with nothing down to how to protect your investment. From how to brand yourself with power to how to pass your legacy to the next generation.

There's a chapter about the neighborhoods people ignore. The ones full of potential, but plagued by systems that want to profit from poverty. You'll learn how to navigate those spaces, how to spot deception, and how to claim what should be given to us, not sold to us at inflated rates.

This is your moment.

Not to be "in the industry" but to be above it.

Not to work for real estate, but to make real estate work for you.

So take a breath.

Open this book like it's a blueprint for your life.

Because it is.

Welcome to the movement.
Welcome to ownership.
Welcome to elevation.

CHAPTER ONE

DON'T WORK REAL ESTATE—OWN IT

Part One

Disrupting The Traditional Career Path In Real Estate

There is a growing belief in communities across the country that if you want to build wealth through real estate, you must first work for someone else to earn your place. They tell you to go to real estate school, get licensed, join a firm, shadow experienced agents, and spend years learning the game one deal at a time. The idea is that one day, after you've closed enough sales and built enough trust, you'll finally be ready to own property yourself. That lie has cost too many people too much time, energy, and dignity.

If you are reading this book, that means you are ready to think differently. You are ready to rise above being someone else's employee and step into the role of owner. You do not need to work in real estate to become wealthy through real estate. That belief is a trap, a carefully designed system that delays your ownership until you've served the goals of others. But if you want to change your life, you need to stop asking how to get hired and start asking how to gain control. You need to stop chasing commissions and start claiming keys. You need to stop working the real estate industry and start working the real estate itself.

Most real estate careers begin with permission. You apply for a license. You take the classes. You wait for your exam results. You submit to someone else's system to prove you are worthy. Then you join a firm, take orders from a broker, split commissions, and follow the internal hierarchy that rewards conformity. You are taught how to smile through rejection, how to dress professionally, how to push listings that may not serve your community or your spirit. But what they do not teach you is how to invest. They do not teach you how to acquire property with no money down. They do not teach you how to think beyond the transaction and into the transformation.

Real estate firms are not designed to make you rich. They are designed to keep you working. There is no freedom in being an agent who needs twenty closings a year just to maintain financial stability. There is no ownership in staying loyal to a company that profits from your hustle while keeping you away from the deed. You may feel close to property, but proximity is not possession. You can sit at the closing table every week and still walk home with nothing.

What they rarely tell you is that you can become an investor without spending years in school or waiting for someone to give you a job. You can learn the language of real estate through books, podcasts, online platforms, mentorship, and study groups. You can position yourself to make deals without having a six-figure savings account. You can access seller financing, lease options, and creative acquisition strategies that don't require approval from banks or brokers. What you need is knowledge, clarity, and courage. What you need is the truth.

And here's a truth too many people avoid: working in real estate can easily become a distraction from owning real estate. You may get caught in the performance. The dress code. The branding. The networking events. You may spend all your energy helping others find homes while watching your own dreams collect dust. You may think success is coming because you are in the room, but the room is a waiting area, not a launchpad.

When you choose ownership, the game changes. You no longer ask for permission. You begin to evaluate properties for yourself. You start negotiating directly with sellers. You ask hard questions about neighborhoods, safety, and legacy. You start thinking about how a property affects your family, your freedom, and your future. You do not rely on market value to determine worth. You do not allow an appraiser to tell you a home is valuable just because the appliances are new and the paint is fresh. You look beyond the surface and ask what others are afraid to see.

Ownership begins with a shift in mindset. It is not about being licensed, it is about being intentional. It is not about helping clients, it is about helping yourself and your community. Ownership means identifying the system that profits from your labor and choosing to opt out. It means seeing the real estate industry not as a path, but as a detour, and deciding to walk your own road.

Many people spend years chasing the title of "agent" or "broker" only to realize they were never taught how to own. The industry taught them how to list, sell, and promote, but not how to buy, protect, and pass on. That is why this book exists. To break that pattern. To challenge the belief that you must earn ownership through someone else's process. To empower you with strategies that allow you to step into property without waiting, without begging, and without fear.

This is the first step. This is the beginning of your elevation. From here, you will learn how to speak the language of ownership, how to navigate the landscape without a license, and how to invest smarter than most professionals ever will.

Part Two

Learn Terminology Not to Serve, But to Invest Smarter

In real estate, language isn't just communication, it's currency. Every contract, negotiation, inspection, appraisal, and transaction is built on terminology. If you don't speak the language, you get locked out of the deal. And unfortunately, many people step into real estate roles believing that fluency in these words should be used to serve clients, not themselves. That mindset is why so many agents stay broke while transactions pass through their hands week after week. They can explain equity, but they haven't built any. They understand mortgage clauses, but they're drowning in one themselves. They know the meaning of "as-is," but have never bought a property for themselves in that condition and capitalized on the opportunity.

That cycle ends here. You don't need to learn real estate terminology to work the system, you need it to outsmart it. Every investor who operates without formal education but knows how to structure creative deals is proof that knowledge, not credentials, makes wealth. When you understand the vocabulary of real estate, you begin seeing options others miss. You start identifying loopholes, restructuring contracts, and asking questions that intimidate sellers and agents who thought you'd be easy to manipulate.

For example, knowing what "subject-to" means allows you to assume an existing mortgage without going through a bank. Knowing what "assignment of contract" means allows you to secure a deal and resell it without ever owning the property physically. Knowing what "ARV" means, after repair value, lets you see not just what a home is worth now, but what it can become with investment. These are not just words, they are keys. And when you learn how to use them, doors open.

Many people avoid studying terminology because they think it's too technical or they've been told they need formal training to understand it. But the truth is, most terminology in real estate is not complex, it's intentionally made to seem that way. Because if the language remains intimidating, then the power remains in the hands of a few. That's why this book breaks down the terms that matter in ways anyone can understand. No fluff. No jargon. Just what you need to read deals like books and negotiate like a seasoned pro.

You don't need a real estate school to become fluent. You need discipline. You need tenacity. And you need access to resources like this one and a few others. There are hundreds of books, online guides, free video tutorials, and podcast episodes that break down terminology in everyday language. The only difference between an investor who closes deals and someone who's waiting to start is that the investor took the time to study. You can do the same, and you must because being ignorant of real estate language costs you in every conversation.

Imagine walking into a negotiation and misunderstanding the word "contingency." That mistake could trap you in a contract you should've exited. Or consider being told a house has "clouded title" and assuming that just means someone else is interested, when in reality, it means the property has unresolved legal issues. Words shape decisions. Words affect money. And if you don't learn the vocabulary, you stay vulnerable.

But when you flip that mindset and say, "I'm not learning this for a career, I'm learning this for control," everything shifts. You no longer feel like you're pretending to be professional. You're functioning as powerful. You're asking questions, rejecting bad deals, rewriting terms, and holding your ground. You don't need to dress like an agent to talk like one. You need to listen, study, write, and apply. Ownership is not about image, it's about literacy.

Educating yourself through language gives you authority. And that authority allows you to walk into rooms where money moves and speak confidently. You don't need a mentor to validate you if the terminology you speak proves you've done the work. That's why one of the first commitments you should make on your ownership journey is to become fluent. Not academically. Strategically.

You don't need to memorize thousands of terms. You need to master the few dozen that come up in every deal. Loan-to-value. Seller concession. Escrow. Comps. Due diligence. Earnest money. Quiet title. These terms repeat. Study them. Write them down. Use flashcards. Apply them in mock scenarios. Speak them out loud with partners or peers. Build your vocabulary until no one can sell you a lie wrapped in a fancy word again.

And most importantly, don't think for one second that this process should only happen in classrooms. Your elevation begins where you sit right now. Whether you're at a kitchen table with a notebook, on a lunch break in your car watching YouTube tutorials, or walking through a neighborhood reading property signs, this is your school. This is your language lab. This is where your empowerment begins.

Part Three

How To Self-Educate Without Formal School Or Firm Dependence

If real estate school were the only pathway to ownership, most of us would never own a single door. Tuition is high. Access is limited. And once enrolled, you're rarely taught how to invest, you're taught how to pass an exam, follow legal procedure, and represent clients within someone else's brokerage. That knowledge might help you pass tests. It won't help you pass down wealth.

The truth is, many of us were never meant to work inside the system. We were meant to challenge it. We were meant to build, restructure, and reclaim, not just participate. That's why you don't need formal education to begin this journey. You need dedication. You need the right materials. And you need to strip away the belief that learning has to be institutional to be powerful.

There are books that cost less than one class credit that will teach you more than a full semester in real estate school. Books written by investors, not just instructors. Books like this one, built from experience, not just theory. And when you combine that with podcasts, free courses, interviews, neighborhood walkthroughs, and personal study, you gain access to a level of truth most licensed professionals never reach.

This is where elevation begins: in the decision to own your knowledge without permission.

You don't need a professor to explain cap rates. You don't need a firm manager to teach you how to talk to motivated sellers. You need time. You need focus. And you need a strategy.

Start by choosing three to five foundational areas of real estate: acquisition, negotiation, rehab, finance, and exit strategies. Study each one intensely. Pick one area each week and dive deep. Build your own curriculum. Watch videos. Take notes. Ask questions. Go beyond the surface and into the mechanics.

Then build your vocabulary. As covered in Part Two, terminology is key. Create flashcards. Write definitions out in your own words. Use them in mock deals. When you can say "I'm considering a subject-to acquisition with seller concessions and delayed closing," you're operating at a level many agents haven't reached.

And just as important as understanding terms is understanding how they move in real time. That means walking neighborhoods. Calling local sellers. Attending city zoning meetings. Asking tough questions at open houses. You don't need credentials to observe value. You need curiosity and courage.

Visit struggling communities. Look past the paint. Look at the schools, the crime rate, the infrastructure. Stand outside the property and listen to the street. Is it quiet, clean, supported or is it broken, dangerous, forgotten? Learn how to appraise like someone who lives the reality, not like someone who profits from the illusion.

The firm won't teach you that. But your mind will, if you let it.

Now take it a step further. Find mentors who are doers, not talkers. People who don't just post deals on social media but explain how they made them happen. Reach out. Ask to walk one property with them. Offer to help document their process. Don't just shadow, engage.

And if no mentor is available, let experience teach you. Run your own mock deals. Drive to five listed properties a week. Pretend you're buying one. Ask the agent questions. Study the way they respond. Learn what they push and what they avoid. Every interaction sharpens your instincts.

Self-education is not a shortcut, it's a blueprint. Because when you control the pace and shape of your learning, you retain ownership of your mind. You're not being taught to conform. You're being trained to elevate.

Understand this: school might teach you how to take a real estate test, but it will never teach you how to buy a home for a dollar. It will never teach you how to negotiate a seller out of a bad mortgage. It will never teach you how to build legacy in forgotten communities. That knowledge comes from your own decision to invest in something deeper, yourself.

You don't need their permission to study. You don't need a classroom to grow. You don't need a firm to validate your journey.

You need books. You need truth. You need time.

And you need to believe this: ownership begins in the mind, long before it shows up in your name.

Part Four

Ownership Begins In Mindset, Not Permission

There's a dangerous belief in underserved communities: the idea that wealth, control, and ownership must be earned through external approval. Many people believe they are not "ready" to own until someone tells them so, whether it's a firm offering them a position, a teacher handing them a certificate, or a banker validating their credit score. But real power doesn't come from permission. It comes from positioning.

When you decide to own, before you're "qualified," before you're accepted, before you're applauded, you shift the entire energy of your life. You stop moving like someone who needs help and start thinking like someone who offers solutions. That doesn't mean you have every tool in place. It means you're building without fear.

Ownership is first and foremost a mindset. It's a refusal to settle for the script handed down by systems designed to benefit themselves. It's not just about having land, it's about cultivating sovereignty over your financial decisions, your goals, and your legacy. You must teach yourself to think as a founder, not a follower. As a negotiator, not a borrower. As a builder, not a beggar.

This shift is emotional, spiritual, and generational. Many of us come from lineages that were never taught the value of property, not because we were incapable, but because we were intentionally excluded. And now, when ownership is finally possible, we're told we must go through ten layers of validation first. That lie is one of the greatest barriers to progress and it's time to burn it along with the mortgage.

You don't need school to see a good deal. You don't need a broker to help you question a rehab's true value. You don't need an agent to tell you a neighborhood is deteriorating when you can see the trash on the curb, hear the school is failing, and watch the block crumble. What you need is confidence, clarity, and the commitment to keep learning.

When you walk into a negotiation, your language matters. But your energy matters more. Your mindset determines how you approach a seller, how you process information, how you respond to inflated prices or shady contracts. If you're thinking like a subordinate, you'll settle. If you're thinking like an owner, you'll challenge.

There are people who have never stepped foot in a classroom and have built portfolios with ten or more properties. They didn't do it through luck, they did it through study, sweat, and strategy. They didn't wait to be told they were ready. They declared it themselves and backed that declaration with relentless execution.

This book is your guide to doing the same. It's not just instruction, it's invitation. An invitation to elevate beyond what the market says, what the agent says, and what your past might suggest. This is about owning your decisions, owning your dignity, and owning your future.

You have already started the journey. You didn't wait for a certification or resume or approval. You picked up a book that challenges what's broken and builds what's possible.

That means you're ready. Not perfect. Not licensed. But prepared. Empowered. Positioned. And from here, we rise.

Part Five

Real Estate Firms Are Not Designed For Your Freedom

When people begin exploring real estate as a career, they are often drawn to the promise of financial opportunity, flexibility, and upward mobility. The billboards advertise success. The social media posts show agents smiling in front of properties. The schools emphasize how many doors are available once you're "licensed to succeed." But the truth beneath the surface is much different. Most people who work in real estate never cross the threshold into ownership. They remain in roles that are designed to serve the system, not to dismantle or transcend it.

Real estate firms thrive by recruiting hard-working people, training them in surface-level information, and pushing them toward high-volume selling. These firms are structured like machines, systems built to feed off your energy and ambition while rarely converting those efforts into personal power. You are taught how to represent buyers and sellers. You are taught how to read contracts, schedule closings, and market listings. But you're not taught how to protect yourself with property. You're not taught how to negotiate for your own benefit. You're taught to carry other people's dreams, not activate your own.

There is no shame in working a job, but there is danger in believing that working inside the real estate system will automatically lead to wealth. That belief has trapped thousands of agents, assistants, coordinators, and transaction processors in cycles of grind with no equity. They may generate commission. They may receive bonuses. But they rarely walk away with ownership and that separation matters more than most will admit.

You must understand the nature of systems built on performance. They are not built to elevate individuals, they are built to sustain productivity. You become part of a process where your value is measured by how well you sell, how well you follow instructions, and how well you meet monthly quotas. If you step outside those metrics, ask the wrong questions, or challenge the firm's authority, you are no longer seen as valuable. You are seen as a problem. And when you are seen as a problem, they push you out of the machine quickly.

Now compare that to ownership. Ownership does not require you to perform for others. It requires you to prepare for yourself. There is no manager tracking your activity. There is no company reviewing your loyalty. There is no industry gatekeeper determining your worth. You operate on your own terms, study at your own pace, and pursue deals that align with your values, not just the bottom line. You are accountable to yourself, your family, and your legacy, not your firm or your quarterly projections.

Ownership also forces you to navigate real decisions. When you own real estate, you face questions that working in real estate rarely prepares you for. You must evaluate neighborhoods honestly. You must analyze not just resale value, but long-term safety, culture, and opportunity. You must develop instincts about contractors, lenders, inspectors, and zoning boards. These are skills that working inside a firm does not teach, because the firm is focused on making sales, not building futures. So while someone working as an agent may close twenty deals a year, they may still lack the wisdom to negotiate a seller-financed acquisition for themselves. They may know how to upsell a rehabbed house, but not how to see through the paint and question the school district, crime stats, or local infrastructure.

That is why you must step away from the belief that working in real estate is enough. It's not. Work will not free you. Ownership will. Work will not elevate your community. Ownership will. Work will not give your children something to inherit. Ownership will.

You must begin viewing firms as training grounds, not destinations. If you choose to work in one, let it be temporary. Let it be strategic. Learn what you need to learn, then leave and apply that knowledge where it counts. Don't waste years hoping someone will reward you with equity. Build the skills required to claim it yourself. Speak the language. Understand the structure. But do it as a student of freedom, not a servant of systems.

Part Six

Declare Your Ownership Before You Acquire It

Ownership is not something you stumble into. It is something you decide. Before the paperwork is signed.

Before the money is sourced. Before the neighborhood is vetted. Real ownership begins the moment you reject the idea that someone else should guide your future. You declare yourself worthy, not based on credentials, but on commitment.

This declaration isn't flashy. It's quiet. It happens in moments where your spirit shifts. When you walk past homes with inflated prices and say, "That's not worth my peace." When you hear a broker speak in circles and you choose to study the terms yourself instead of being led. When you step into a room and don't ask if you belong, you start asking what deal you're willing to make on your own terms.

That's when the elevation starts.

What you carry now, as a reader and a future investor, is more than curiosity, it's power. The kind of power that comes from seeing systems clearly. From understanding that not all education is designed to free you. That not all guidance is built to lift you. And that your greatest breakthroughs will not come through approval, they will come through action.

If you've made it this far into Chapter One, you've already rejected the traditional path. You no longer believe that working inside a real estate firm automatically leads to wealth. You don't mistake industry jargon for wisdom. You've seen behind the curtain and you're not intimidated by what's back there.

You're ready to build your own strategy.

From here, your role is to keep learning on purpose. Read the books, take the notes, ask the questions that scare gatekeepers. Surround yourself with those who don't need applause to succeed. Visit communities others ignore. Walk through open houses like you're the owner, not a spectator. Rewrite the rules of engagement so that the power never sits outside you again.

And understand this deeply: ownership is not just about property. It's about identity. It's about claiming space in a world that would rather rent your value than invest in it. It's about walking through neighborhoods they told you to avoid and saying, "We can build here. But we won't be robbed by cute illusions and broken promises."

That home with fresh paint but no working school nearby, that is not an asset. That home staged to look modern but surrounded by danger, that is not your dream. The agent telling you the price is fair because the cabinets were updated, that is not your truth. Your truth is protection. Your truth is legacy. Your truth is negotiation rooted in knowledge, not desperation.

So what's next?

You read every chapter with intention. You study the vocabulary not to impress, but to execute. You structure deals that reflect not just your ambition, but your values. You ask sellers hard questions. You walk away from scams with grace. You rebuild your confidence in every deal that puts you closer to land, closer to freedom, closer to generational impact.

And when it's time to act, you will not hesitate. You will not shrink. You will not overpay. You will not be fooled by cosmetic renovation in a neighborhood that hasn't earned your investment. You will remember what this chapter taught you:

Do not work real estate—own it.

Do not chase permission—build position.

Do not be impressed by the system—rewrite it.

The path is now yours. Let's walk it with clarity, with fire, and with full ownership of what comes next.

CHAPTER TWO

THE LANGUAGE OF OWNERSHIP

Part One

Mastering Real Estate Terms As Your First Investment Tool

Before you purchase your first property, before you negotiate your first deal, before you rehab, flip, rent, or leverage anything, you must learn the language. Not academically. Not to impress anyone. But to equip yourself with the tools to protect your value, defend your decisions, and elevate your results. Real estate terminology is your first weapon, your first shield, your first blueprint. And it is often the difference between someone who gets a raw deal and someone who walks away with power.

In marginalized communities, the language of real estate is often withheld, distorted, or used against the buyer. Terms are tossed around casually, ARV, escrow, subject-to, lien, equity, comp, cap rate and if you don't know what they mean, you risk agreeing to something dangerous or walking away from something that could have changed your life. You can't afford that risk. You must study it like your freedom depends on it, because in many cases, it does.

You don't need to memorize every word in a dictionary. But you do need to understand the key terms that shape every deal: how they move, how they protect, how they deceive, and how they empower. When someone says "seller concession," you need to hear opportunity. When someone says "clouded title," you need to hear caution. When someone says "assignable contract," you need to hear flexibility. These are not just definitions. They are strategies disguised as vocabulary.

Take "wholesaling" for example. A word that many agents and institutions barely mention, but it's a cornerstone of creative investing. Wholesaling is the process of securing a contract for a property and selling that contract to another buyer, often without using your own money. Know the word, master the strategy. But without the language, it looks like a hustle, something risky or vague. With the language, it becomes legal, powerful, and life-changing.

Understanding terminology also gives you confidence in rooms where you're expected to shrink. You're no longer the silent buyer. You're no longer the unsure mentee. You're the one who asks direct questions, interprets the answers, and makes decisions without hesitation. You don't wait for someone to explain the details, you've already studied them.

When you read listings, you know what "as-is" means. You know what "motivated seller" might indicate. You know what "cash buyers only" implies about condition and lender limitations. You decode the message behind the words and that means you are in control.

This chapter exists to give you that control.

Because when you speak the language of ownership, you don't just participate, you lead. You don't just ask questions, you set terms. You don't just receive information, you evaluate it. And when someone tries to fast-talk you into a bad deal, you stop them cold, with clarity, precision, and calm strength.

Part Two

Book-Based Learning, Podcasts, Mentors—Resources That Build Your Vocabulary

There's no institution, title, or job role that determines whether someone becomes fluent in the language of real estate. Fluency comes from exposure, repetition, and relentless curiosity. If formal education isn't accessible, the world is filled with alternate pathways, paths that aren't just effective, they're often more honest. Because real estate school may teach you the legal frameworks and definitions, but it rarely prepares you to invest. It doesn't teach you to ask hard questions. It doesn't show you how deals actually move through distressed communities or how buyers in underserved areas navigate negotiation with limited cash. That kind of knowledge comes from self-guided study, direct mentorship, and listening to real-world voices who've done it with grit, not a syllabus.

Books are the most accessible and reliable tools for vocabulary building. They don't interrupt your learning with ads, gatekeep your access with tuition fees, or dilute the message to keep sponsors happy. Books go deep. Books can be revisited. Books don't rush you. And for someone ready to claim ownership on their own terms, reading is not a chore, it's fuel. There are books that break down terminology in plain language, books that chronicle real investor case studies, and books that show how certain phrases, like "earnest money," "subject-to," or "wraparound mortgage" can be used strategically in deals that cost zero up front. You learn from these texts not just what the words mean, but how to move in real time using them.

Podcasts and audio interviews are another resource. The benefit of audio is that you hear confidence in the speaker's delivery. You hear hesitation. You hear details that don't make it into textbooks. Real investors and educators use these platforms to share insights that emerge during live deals. You'll often learn more terminology from a twenty-minute episode featuring a successful investor walking through an acquisition than you will from a three-hour classroom lecture focused on test preparation. And because podcasts are mobile, they allow you to study while driving, walking, cooking, or even scouting neighborhoods. In the elevation journey, efficiency matters. Audio lets you study without slowing down your life.

Mentorship, both formal and informal, is the accelerator. Not every mentor wears a title or works in a firm. Many are quiet builders. Landlords who started by buying one home. Wholesalers who closed deals while still working full-time jobs. Rehabbers who rebuilt two houses before ever advertising their services. These people are loaded with vocabulary, they just may not call it that. But when you ask questions, their responses contain lessons in every sentence. They'll tell you what clauses to look for in contracts. They'll tell you how the term "option period" can protect you during inspections. They'll mention "double closing" in a casual story, and if you're paying attention, you'll walk away with a brand-new strategy.

To access mentorship, you don't have to beg or feel beneath anyone. You observe, you offer value, and you stay ready to absorb. Attend community investment meetings. Ask if you can walk a property with someone who's active. Volunteer to document a rehab. Share their work in exchange for a look behind the scenes. Be clear that you're there to learn, not to copy or compete. Most people are willing to share information with those who demonstrate respect and hunger. And if a mentor teaches you the meaning of just five new terms, especially ones they use regularly, you've grown your vocabulary in a way no institution can replicate.

Part Three

Why Knowing The Language Levels The Playing Field

In every transaction, every contract, every discussion about property, language shapes power. When you don't know the vocabulary of real estate, you are negotiating in the dark. You may think you're making a fair deal, but you're not fully equipped to protect yourself. You may believe you're asking the right questions, but the answers you're given are often framed to exploit your lack of fluency. The gap in language is one of the most effective ways the real estate system preserves inequality.

The industry thrives on selective access. If you don't understand what "quiet title" means, you won't catch the legal risks attached to the property. If you don't know the impact of "loan-to-value ratio," you might not realize you're walking into a deal that puts you in immediate financial stress. If you can't interpret "due diligence period" correctly, you might miss the window to exit a contract before it locks you down. Every term you fail to know becomes a window for someone else to profit from your confusion.

And this is not random. Systems are built this way intentionally. If everyone knew how to interpret comps, calculate ARV, or challenge inflated appraisals, the manipulation would collapse. People wouldn't overpay for properties with superficial upgrades in broken communities. They wouldn't settle for predatory loan terms or buy homes they can't realistically rehab. Knowledge disrupts cycles and language is the first layer of that knowledge.

Once you begin speaking with clarity, the dynamic shifts. You're no longer treated like a passive buyer, you're seen as a peer. And while some may feel threatened by that, others will respect it. You'll notice agents adjust how they pitch listings. You'll notice sellers hesitate before overstating a property's value. You'll notice lenders speak more carefully when explaining rates. Because when you understand the language, you activate authority. You demonstrate that you're not here to play, you're here to negotiate.

This becomes especially important in communities targeted by investor vultures. Areas where property is undervalued, but marketed as "emerging." Where cosmetic rehabs are used to inflate asking prices, while the surrounding environment remains neglected. These deals are often pushed on buyers who've never been taught how to appraise from a community standpoint. But if you walk in knowing the right words, if you question the zoning, the comps, the infrastructure, and the seller's reasoning—you no longer fit the profile of the easy target. You've just leveled the field.

The truth is, language creates access where money can't. You may not have capital yet, but if you have vocabulary, you have leverage. You can approach sellers with structured offers. You can challenge terms others accept blindly. You can walk away from bad deals and close smart ones, because the words you're speaking are rooted in clarity, not compliance.

Part Four

Owning The Conversation—Disarming Intimidation Through Fluency

In the world of real estate, there's more than a power imbalance, it's a language barrier dressed as legitimacy. Walk into any high-stakes negotiation or investment meeting, and the words flying around the room are designed to separate those who belong from those who merely showed up. Agents, lenders, sellers, appraisers, they speak a dialect rooted in profit, paperwork, and legal nuance. If you're not fluent, you're vulnerable. You might be present, but you're not positioned.

This barrier is intentional. Real estate systems are built to preserve privilege and protect insiders. The average first-time buyer isn't taught how to counter inflated appraisals, recognize misleading comps, or dispute zoning manipulations. Instead, they're overwhelmed by unfamiliar vocabulary, terms stacked against them not because the buyer lacks intelligence, but because the industry thrives when the buyer lacks access.

But when you learn the language, you start to dismantle the intimidation. The same words that once made you second-guess your instincts become tools in your arsenal. You hear "ARV," and you ask what rehab assumptions were used. You hear "cash buyers only," and you understand the structural limitations or title complications involved. You hear "clouded title," and you know to slow down, call a specialist, and protect your investment. Vocabulary transforms from obstacle to leverage.

When you speak fluently, tone shifts. You're no longer treated as a passive participant. Sellers adjust their pitches. Agents clarify their numbers. Lenders lean in, calculating their responses carefully. You've disrupted the default assumption that you're uninformed. This disruption isn't just psychological, it's tactical. The more precise your language, the fewer shortcuts they can take in your presence.

That's the power of applied fluency. You don't just understand terms, you use them to interrogate deals, defend your interests, and keep decision-makers honest. You don't wait for explanations, you provide alternatives. You don't absorb pressure, you redirect it. And whether you're walking through a duplex on the edge of gentrification or sitting across from a banker explaining your strategy for a subject-to purchase, you control the narrative.

There's another layer here. Fluency affects how you speak to your own community. Many potential buyers come from neighborhoods where the terminology of ownership is absent. They weren't raised hearing words like "escrow," "quiet title," "seller financing," or "wraparound mortgage." And when they begin their journey, they're often ridiculed for not being "ready." But when you speak the language clearly, you become the bridge. You explain terms without arrogance. You translate opportunity. You educate as you elevate. And that changes everything.

Real estate intimidation isn't just about money, it's about perception. But when your vocabulary matches your vision, perception collapses. You walk into rooms built to confuse, and you rearrange them with clarity.

Part Five

Practicing Fluency Until Precision Becomes Instinct

Mastering vocabulary is not about memorizing lists, it's about using the language so naturally, no one questions your authority. That level of fluency doesn't come from passively reading definitions. It comes from repetition, rehearsal, and immersion. You must train your tongue to speak the terms clearly. You must practice inserting key phrases into negotiation mockups. You must engage in scenarios where vocabulary isn't just referenced, it drives decisions.

The transformation begins when these terms move off the page and into daily use. When you walk a property and instinctively evaluate its ARV and demand to see the comps. When you look at a purchase agreement and immediately scan for clauses governing option periods, termination rights, and earnest money safeguards. You begin to operate with a precision that others recognize as seasoned, even if you've never worked inside a firm.

Start building your fluency like a workout regimen. Identify twenty essential terms, ones that shape 90% of real estate negotiations and contracts. These might include: subject-to, wraparound mortgage, seller financing, equity, comps, contingency, escrow, due diligence, assignable contracts, lien, clouded title, ARV, cash buyer, loan-to-value, amortization, and more. Write them down. Define them in your own language. Don't settle for textbook interpretations, translate them into action. Then use them out loud.

Create mock negotiations with partners or mentors. Walk through a fictional deal where you structure a seller-financed purchase with no money down. Draft mock contracts using real templates available online. Call local agents and ask questions as if you're preparing to buy, listen to how they speak and note how your responses evolve over time. The goal isn't to impress, it's to prepare. When the real negotiation arrives, you'll be ready not because you memorized the material, but because you lived it.

Fluency also means knowing when silence is a trap. If someone speeds through a deal and skips key terminology, that's your cue to interrupt. If a lender starts quoting numbers without unpacking the source assumptions, that's your moment to reframe the conversation. When you're fluent, confusion doesn't intimidate you, it activates you.

Language also influences your leadership in group discussions. Many real estate deals involve multiple parties. Whether you're collaborating on a community project or partnering on an investment, your vocabulary sets the tone. If you speak with clarity, others will defer to your analysis. If you interpret clauses others overlook, you become the strategist. This builds trust. It builds credibility. And most importantly, it builds confidence within your team and your circle.

To reach this level, schedule vocabulary review into your routine. Ten minutes a day. Quiz yourself. Speak terms aloud while walking your own neighborhood. Watch YouTube videos of investors breaking down deals and pause to repeat phrases back. Real estate fluency isn't just about what you know, it's about what you've internalized so deeply, no one can take it from you.

Every deal you study, every term you use, every clause you question strengthens your position. You aren't studying to pass a test—you're studying to walk into spaces where you were once denied and close deals without flinching. Vocabulary sharpens vision. Practice breeds precision. And the confidence that follows will be built not on titles—but on truth.

Part Six

Building Your Investment Identity Through Language

Real estate vocabulary doesn't just prepare you for transactions, it shapes how you see yourself in the financial world. When your mouth speaks terms with precision, your mind begins to see possibilities with clarity. And when your daily language reflects strategic thinking, your entire investment identity evolves. You stop reacting to opportunities, you begin crafting them.

This shift starts in ordinary moments. When you overhear someone mention a refinance, and you immediately analyze the terms they accepted. When someone brags about buying a home, and your first question is whether they secured seller concessions or overpaid based on inflated comps. You're no longer just a participant in conversation, you're the voice others start turning to when they need answers they can trust.

Identity in real estate is rarely discussed, but it's everywhere. Your presence, your tone, your questions, all signal whether you are there to be sold or to do the buying. Fluency reinforces that signal. It communicates that you read more than headlines, that you don't flinch at closing documents, and that your curiosity isn't passive, it's tactical. You become known not just as someone who talks real estate, but someone who thinks in equity, negotiates through protection, and moves with strategic clarity.

This reputation isn't built overnight. It's built through consistency. Use every interaction as practice. Every phone call with a lender becomes a vocabulary drill. Every open house becomes a case study. Every podcast you listen to becomes an opportunity to expand your interpretation. You aren't just absorbing information, you're rewriting your internal blueprint. And that blueprint will guide how you evaluate neighborhoods, how you assess risk, and how you build legacy.

Language also affects the spaces you access. If you can speak fluently across real estate functions, development, finance, legal, investment, you'll be welcomed into conversations that shape cities, not just listings. You'll meet builders, funders, and organizers who respect your insights, because your terminology reveals that you don't just attend meetings, you shift them. You become a thinker whose opinions carry weight, because they're grounded in fluency, not fluff.

That identity transcends property. It follows you into every sphere. You'll be invited to speak, consult, and collaborate. Your vocabulary becomes your brand. Your clarity becomes your marketing. And your authority becomes the doorway to partnerships, investment opportunities, and financial expansion that others thought required credentials.

But you didn't need the certificate. You needed precision. You didn't need a badge. You needed consistency. You didn't need permission. You needed language and now that you've claimed it, elevation becomes your default setting.

Part Seven

Breaking Cultural Barriers Through Terminology Empowerment

For generations, real estate conversations have excluded voices from communities where property was treated as inaccessible, irrelevant, or even dangerous. The language of ownership was rarely spoken around kitchen tables in neighborhoods facing systemic disinvestment. Most of the dialogue centered on rent, eviction, relocation, or survival, not strategy, leverage, or legacy. This omission wasn't accidental, it was structured. By withholding terminology, institutions made it harder for marginalized families to see property as a tool rather than a trap. So when you begin mastering real estate vocabulary, you're not just learning a skill, you're recovering a right.

Breaking that cultural barrier requires more than individual study, it demands reintroduction. You must walk back into spaces where ownership language was never present and begin speaking it aloud. That could mean explaining "seller financing" to a family member who's always assumed banks were the only path. It could mean teaching a young person what "ARV" means, not just as a calculation, but as a vision for community rehabilitation. It could mean translating terms that seem complex, like "equitable interest" into real-world scenarios that feel relevant to people who have never thought property belonged to them.

This work is slow, but it's powerful. When you begin demystifying vocabulary in your circles, you do more than educate, you liberate. You help others imagine lives where ownership isn't reserved for someone with a suit or a license. You anchor value where it belongs: in clarity, in control, and in community. And the more people around you begin using the terms you've studied, the more those terms become tools for local empowerment.

Consider what happens when an entire block begins using real estate language confidently. Neighbors share deal insights. They question city zoning together. They assess developer plans with precision. They meet investors on equal footing. The vocabulary becomes common, and common language births collective action. That's how neighborhoods shift, from renters waiting for change to stakeholders orchestrating it.

Fluency also changes how you see opportunity. Before, a vacant home on your street might have represented blight. Now, you recognize its potential because you understand how to structure a creative acquisition, how to finance its rehab, and how to project its resale or rental value. Language lets you move from passive observation to strategic activation. You don't just watch neighborhoods transform, you guide the transformation.

But none of this happens through theory alone. It happens through relentless communication. You must speak the terms until they're familiar. Practice explaining complex strategies in language accessible to someone with no background. Invite questions and answer them without condescension. Share resources. Build vocabulary circles. Treat ownership fluency as a form of cultural restoration.

This work affirms that real estate isn't just for investors, it's for visionaries who dare to redefine value from the ground up.

Final Part

From Fluency To Financial Sovereignty

The journey from terminology to transformation is not just about being able to speak in real estate code, it's about using that fluency to build financial sovereignty. That means owning decisions, navigating systems without submission, and turning words into wealth-generating strategies that don't rely on gatekeepers. Every term you've learned in this chapter is a doorway into an investment conversation. But it's what you do with that doorway, how you step through it, how you frame your goals, how you protect your assets, that determines your future.

Financial sovereignty begins when you stop using language to survive deals and start using it to engineer them. You no longer wait for options to be handed to you—you identify them, structure them, and present them on your own terms. You might approach a seller with a subject-to proposal, pairing creative finance with community uplift. You might challenge a realtor's pricing with a data-backed comp analysis that incorporates crime index, school performance, and long-term zoning impacts. You might walk into a closing with enough confidence in your documentation to renegotiate escrow allocations. These moves aren't magic, they're manifestations of mastery.

The system has long depended on our silence. On our hesitation. On our belief that we need to work real estate instead of own it. But fluency disrupts that dependency. It allows you to read 100 pages of a contract and not blink. It lets you absorb conversations with lenders and hear what's not being said. It gives you the clarity to walk away from a deal that looks tempting but lacks integrity. You build rhythm. You build resilience. And you build respect, not because you have a title, but because your language demands it.

Sovereignty also means setting boundaries. You reject deals that violate your principles. You refuse offers that look profitable but compromise community safety. You recognize that ownership without dignity is not ownership, it's exploitation dressed up in fancy paperwork. So you create strategies that reflect your soul, not just your spreadsheets.

And then, you teach. You pass your language to others, not diluted, not oversimplified, but strengthened through shared use. You help your child understand what ARV means before they reach high school. You walk your neighbor through a contract they would've been afraid to sign alone. You drop knowledge in barbershops, family gatherings, and online posts, not for attention, but for elevation.

Because that's what fluency gives you: the power to rewrite economic narratives, not just for yourself, but for everyone watching.

You've now built your foundation. The vocabulary isn't just a list, it's a mindset. A declaration. A weapon.

And it's time to use it.

CHAPTER THREE

GAME THE SYSTEM: INVESTING WITH NO MONEY DOWN

Part One

Seller Financing, Subject-To, And The Architecture Of Creative Contracts

Investing without capital isn't a fantasy, it's a methodology. One the system doesn't want you to understand, because once you master it, you stop asking for loans. You stop chasing pre-approvals. You stop worrying whether your credit score will open the door. You learn how to build deals not on dollars, but on language, strategy, and leverage.

At the heart of no-money-down investing lies creative financing. That doesn't mean you scam your way into ownership. It means you structure deals based on mutual advantage rather than institutional approval. And there are three primary approaches: seller financing, subject-to transactions, and creative contracts. Each one bypasses the traditional lender gate and repositions the buyer as a negotiator rather than an applicant.

Seller financing is the most straightforward. The seller acts as the bank, allowing you to purchase the property directly without involving a lender. You agree to a price, a payment schedule, and a set of terms. Instead of wiring funds from a mortgage company, you begin monthly payments to the seller themselves. This method is often used in situations where the seller owns the property free and clear and is willing to receive steady income rather than a lump sum.

The power in seller financing comes from flexibility. You negotiate terms based on your actual situation, not formulas imposed by institutions. You can structure deferred payments. You can build in renovation contingencies. You can include performance-based clauses where payment terms shift based on what improvements you make to the property. In this setup, clarity and trust matter more than credentials. You don't need a pre-approval letter, you need a persuasive strategy and the ability to honor your word.

Subject-to transactions are more complex, but equally powerful. In this scenario, you take ownership of a property while leaving the existing mortgage in place. The seller allows you to assume responsibility for the mortgage payments, but the loan remains in their name. You gain control of the property, operate it as your own, and pay the note monthly. The lender is not notified or asked for permission, hence the term "subject to" the existing financing.

This structure is ideal when the seller is struggling and wants relief from payments but doesn't want to go through foreclosure or wait on a traditional sale. You step in, take over the burden, and start controlling the asset immediately. Your challenge is to manage the relationship carefully. Because while you're paying the mortgage, the original owner's name is still on paper. That means you must protect the deal with performance. No missed payments. No disrespect. No recklessness. When done correctly, subject-to deals are lightning rods for elevation. They require almost no upfront cash but unlock full access to equity, cash flow, and property control.

Creative contracts are the hybrid approach. These include lease options, option-to-purchase agreements, land contracts, and other deal structures where ownership transfers are delayed, contingent, or staged. These methods are perfect when you want to enter a deal, improve the asset, and then close once your liquidity improves. You lock in terms early, secure legal ground to occupy or improve the property, and activate your strategy in phases.

None of these methods are taught in traditional real estate school. They are intentionally buried under layers of formal training, paperwork, and discouragement. Because if buyers begin using creative structures routinely, the mortgage industry loses power. Title companies lose exclusivity. Loan officers lose commission. That's why this book pulls back the curtain. These strategies are not reserved for elite investors, they are tools for anyone who studies, applies, and walks in with vision.

Part Two

How Broke Investors Make Powerful Plays

The myth that you need capital to start in real estate is one of the most effective lies the industry has ever told. It's repeated often and confidently, usually by people selling courses, gatekeeping access, or guarding their own seat at the table. And it convinces thousands of potential owners to delay action, waiting for a day when their savings account will finally qualify them to dream. But here's the truth: every week, broke investors are closing deals. Not because they hit the lottery, but because they studied what others ignored. They moved creatively. They spoke fluently. They made plays rooted in strategy, not bank approval.

Being broke doesn't mean being powerless. It means you must trade what you lack in capital for what you can cultivate in credibility, hustle, and clarity. Deals move because someone believes in your ability to execute, not just your ability to wire funds. And if you study long enough, you'll find that most sellers are less concerned about your bank balance than they are about their peace of mind. If you can offer solutions, structure mutually beneficial terms, and manage a closing with competence, many will choose you over buyers with deeper pockets but weaker follow-through.

The most successful broke investors master two things: information and timing. They study properties others overlook, and they move when sellers are most open to creative terms. That means targeting vacant homes, distressed owners, probate listings, and off-market opportunities. These are situations where the seller isn't thinking about bidding wars, they're thinking about relief. And if you show up with answers, not excuses, you are already ahead.

Let's break it down further.

Say you find a property where the seller has inherited a home they don't want. It's outdated. It needs work. It's been sitting for months. You don't have the cash to buy it outright. But you've done your homework. You approach the seller and offer a subject-to structure: you'll take over their existing mortgage payments, handle the rehab, and work toward either resale or rental, all without them needing to lift another finger. You present a written plan, reference your network, and set a timeline. Suddenly, the seller sees you not as a risky buyer, but as an answer to a problem.

Or imagine you locate a landlord who's tired of managing a property. Tenants have been late. Repairs have stacked up. They're ready to exit. You offer seller financing, with no money down, but you include a clause that allows the seller to retain partial interest for the first 12 months, earning passive income while you stabilize the asset. You showcase your plan for maintenance and cash flow. You promise professional management and transparency. You're not showing cash, you're showing capacity.

These deals happen every day. They just don't get advertised on TV. They're quiet transactions, often closed over coffee, phone calls, or handwritten agreements. And the investors behind them are rarely rich. They're resourceful.

But let's be honest: being broke comes with pressure. You may feel behind. You may feel invisible. You may feel like every deal you approach is one bad credit check away from falling through. That's why your mindset must be rooted in discipline. You don't chase every lead, you pursue the ones where creativity matters most. You don't overpromise, you over-prepare. You speak plainly, document thoroughly, and always operate with integrity. Because credibility is currency when money is missing.

And when you stack successful deals through resourcefulness, your reputation begins to build. Sellers talk. Communities pay attention. Mentors take notice. Suddenly, you're the investor others want to learn from, not because you had the most capital, but because you made the best moves with the least conventional tools.

Part Three

Building Credibility Without Capital

In real estate, credibility moves deals long before capital does. Sellers don't just look for buyers, they look for confidence. They want assurance that whoever steps into their property will follow through, protect their interest, and operate with integrity. That means if you show up broke but prepared, you stand a stronger chance than someone who shows up rich but reckless. Building credibility without capital is not a trick, it's a skillset rooted in communication, documentation, and strategic presence.

First, study every part of the process so you never fumble language. When you speak with precision about title structure, lien searches, contingency clauses, and financing alternatives, it signals that you're not casually exploring, you're actively executing. Sellers hear your knowledge and immediately begin adjusting their perception. You're no longer just a buyer, you're an operator. You know how to identify value, secure property, manage expectations, and deliver results. That impression is priceless.

Second, build a presentation framework. This can be as simple as a typed one-pager or as elaborate as a PDF proposal. It should include your investment philosophy, your goals, your strategy for the property, and a timeline for execution. Show them how you plan to secure tenants, manage repairs, improve curb appeal, or navigate the resale.

You don't need graphics or logos, you need clarity. When a seller sees your plan laid out, it lowers anxiety and builds trust. You're telling them: I may not have the funds now, but I have the focus. I've done the work. I'm already moving.

You also need to have an answer for every risk they may perceive. If they ask what happens if your financing falls through, explain your backup plan. If they worry about deferred payments, offer protective clauses that give them recourse. If they're hesitant about signing over control, walk them through exit options, performance markers, and legal protections. You aren't just negotiating, you're managing emotion. And every reassurance you provide becomes part of your credibility portfolio.

Documentation matters here. Bring example contracts. Walk them through a previous deal you studied, even if you weren't directly involved. Show them how you interpret legal language. Show them how you break down deal metrics. Show them how you protect sellers while still activating your ownership strategy. You are there to lead the deal, not just sign it.

Next, leverage relationships. If you've worked alongside contractors, agents, title companies, or mentors, even in an unofficial capacity, refer to them. Reference conversations, training, and shared learning experiences. Sellers want to know you're not navigating alone. You may be new, but you're not isolated. You've built your approach in community. And community builds stability.

Then, speak with integrity. That doesn't mean making yourself sound polished, it means making yourself sound honest. Don't inflate your resources. Don't exaggerate your network. Don't pretend you've closed ten deals if you're still on your first one. Say what you know. Say what you don't. Say how you plan to learn the rest. When you show humility backed by preparation, it disarms resistance. You become a trustworthy participant in a system known for its smoke and mirrors.

Finally, follow through. If you set a meeting time, arrive early. If you promise paperwork, deliver it on time. If you say you'll call with an update, call without delay. Every small execution builds your brand as a serious operator. You are showing the seller, in action, that you honor process even when money isn't flowing yet. That level of diligence transforms skepticism into partnership.

Because at the end of the day, credibility closes deals where cash cannot. And when your name becomes associated with strategy, honesty, and precision, you unlock more doors than money ever could.

Part Four

Reshaping Communities Through Ownership Without Capital

No-money-down strategies aren't just clever financial maneuvers, they're tools for reimagining entire communities. When investors with little to no capital begin closing deals using seller financing, subject-to arrangements, and creative contracts, they do more than prove a point, they challenge the gatekeeping of generational wealth. And when these strategies enter overlooked neighborhoods, they don't just disrupt industry norms, they reclaim real estate as a vehicle for restoration, equity, and local control.

These communities, often framed by cycles of disinvestment and external speculation, have been told for decades that ownership isn't feasible. Banks redlined them. Appraisers undervalued them. Developers manipulated them. And residents were expected to either rent forever or leave. Yet these very spaces hold some of the strongest potential for no-money-down acquisition. Why? Because sellers are present, problems are visible, and solutions, when offered with respect and strategy, are welcome.

Take a block full of inherited properties. Elderly owners hold homes they no longer want, no longer maintain, or no longer live in. They've tried listing them, but buyers backed out. Or they've avoided listing altogether out of fear, grief, or lack of support. Now imagine an investor approaching one of those owners not with cash, but with clarity. Offering a seller-financed exit plan. Proposing a community-minded rehab strategy. Ensuring the home won't be flipped and abandoned, but secured and strengthened. Suddenly, that conversation isn't about money, it's about meaning. That's how deals shift from transactional to transformational.

When these methods are used collectively, the impact multiplies. One no-money-down acquisition might stabilize a property. Ten can reshape a neighborhood. And when those deals are informed by language, integrity, and genuine care, they don't just activate profit, they restore pride. Communities begin to see themselves not as renters or survivors, but as stakeholders and strategists.

But this requires intentional movement. Investors using no-money-down strategies must operate with more than individual ambition. They must apply these tactics with awareness of the histories, traumas, and potential embedded in the places they invest. That means choosing deals that honor people, not just spreadsheets. That means using terms like "equitable interest" and "wraparound mortgage" not to confuse others but to teach, mentor, and guide. That means understanding that real estate is never just about walls, it's about the story behind them.

No-money-down investing also opens doors for people who've long felt excluded. Younger investors. Renters ready to transition. Parents with big dreams but small budgets. Entrepreneurs without collateral. These individuals carry vision and creative strategy gives them the infrastructure to materialize it. Now, instead of waiting five years to save a down payment, they spend five months studying subject-to deals. Instead of begging banks for approval, they secure seller trust through documentation and dialogue. The playing field isn't just being leveled, it's being reclaimed.

This shift creates new models of mentorship. Investors who've closed deals with no cash now have authority to teach others how to move with precision. They host workshops. Share resources. Co-invest with peers. They show that owning with strategy isn't a loophole, it's a liberation.

Part Five

Scaling Without Cash—Creative Leverage and Strategic Expansion

Once you've proven that ownership doesn't require capital, the natural next question is: How far can you take it? One deal is empowering. Two build momentum. But when you apply creative financing at scale, you redefine what it means to be a real estate investor entirely. You stop chasing occasional wins and begin engineering long-term growth, portfolio expansion, cash flow generation, and strategic partnerships, all fueled by leveraged structures rather than liquid assets.

Creative leverage begins by mastering repeatable frameworks. If you closed your first deal through seller financing, document that process down to every detail: how you found the seller, how you structured the terms, how you built trust, and how you navigated the close. Turn that into your personal playbook. Now apply that same template to the next deal, adjusting for the seller's personality, the property's quirks, and your evolving timeline. The goal is to replicate success without starting from scratch each time.

Subject-to transactions scale differently. These deals rely on identifying sellers with active mortgages and willingness to transfer ownership while keeping financing in place. To scale this, create a system for locating distressed homeowners, those behind on payments, going through divorce, relocating for work, or dealing with inherited liabilities. You can tap into public records, network with probate attorneys, or drive target neighborhoods looking for signs of distress. Build outreach strategies grounded in empathy and precision. You're not hunting for vulnerability, you're offering resolution.

Land contracts and lease options offer additional scaling tools. These arrangements allow you to secure control of multiple properties through staged agreements, often requiring little to no upfront cash. For lease options, focus on owners struggling to sell, offer to lease with intent to buy after twelve to twenty-four months. Structure those agreements with predetermined purchase prices, clear timelines, and repair clauses that allow you to improve the property while delaying full acquisition. Each deal adds one more door to your portfolio, building equity while preserving liquidity.

Partnerships emerge as your visibility increases. When peers see you closing deals creatively and ethically, they'll want in, not because you have the most money, but because you have the most strategy. These collaborations can take many forms: joint ventures where you bring the structure and they bring the funding, mentorships where you help others close their first deal, or networks where resources are pooled to secure larger assets. The power lies in alignment. You don't need everyone, you need the right few who believe in your playbook and respect your process.

Cash flow expands from these deals in stages. Some properties offer immediate rental income. Others may need rehab, tenant placement, or refinancing. Because you've conserved capital on the acquisition, you can reinvest your revenue strategically. Whether it's funding small renovations, marketing new deals, or strengthening operational systems, each dollar flows from equity, not debt. That's the difference between creative scale and conventional scale: you grow without drowning in loan obligations or investor demands.

This kind of expansion also shifts how communities perceive ownership. You become a presence, not just a participant. You help stabilize properties, improve blocks, and inspire others to learn and replicate. Your deals stop being isolated wins, they become proofs of possibility. And when no-money-down strategies ripple outward, entire neighborhoods start believing in their ability to control, protect, and elevate.

Part Six

Mastering Your Narrative—Positioning Strategy as Authority

When you operate without capital, what closes the gap isn't charisma or luck, it's your narrative. Every interaction with a seller, lender, partner, or peer becomes an opportunity to frame your story as strategy. If you want the deal, but lack the down payment, you must offer clarity stronger than cash. You're not asking for pity, you're presenting precision. Your narrative becomes your business card, your investor profile, and your protection against doubt.

This starts with truth. You acknowledge where you're at financially, without apology or defensiveness. You affirm what you've studied, the strategies you're applying, and the partners you're building with. You present your model not as a workaround, but as a calculated system grounded in transparency and execution. You explain why subject-to deals preserve seller dignity. You break down how seller financing generates passive income for the seller while allowing you to secure property without third-party debt. You illustrate how creative contracts minimize risk and maximize control for everyone involved. And you do it without rushing, without overselling, and without trying to sound more accomplished than you are.

Your authority stems from structure. Every step in your process is documented. You carry binders, folders, PDFs, or digital portfolios that showcase your readiness. You've built offer templates. You've prepared scripts. You've rehearsed key conversations and legal clauses. When you walk into a meeting, no one has to wonder what your role is. You speak like a builder, because you are one. You speak like an owner, because you're becoming one. You position your lack of cash as irrelevant, because your presence is abundant, with knowledge, direction, and clarity.

The strongest investors without capital are not trying to be impressive, they're trying to be accurate. They know that bluffing undermines deals. They've learned that clarity beats confidence when trust is on the line. They've witnessed transactions fall apart because one party prioritized image over substance. That's why they approach every meeting with three intentions: educate, empower, and execute.

Education means being able to explain your deal without jargon or panic. You walk the seller through each clause, showing where protections lie, where flexibility exists, and how exit strategies are embedded. Empowerment means giving the seller room to respond, never cornering them, never rushing them, but guiding them with firm respect. Execution means knowing your next move before the current one closes. You're already thinking about contractors, permits, rental strategy, or resale. You're not just acquiring, you're activating.

This positioning ripples outward. It affects how your name is spoken. Sellers refer you not as "the one with no money," but "the one who gets it done." Partners describe you as "the strategist," not "the struggler." You've reframed your identity through preparation. And the more you operate this way, the less anyone cares how much cash you brought to the table, because your value is already on it.

Final Part

Beyond the Deal—Sustaining Ownership and Building the Legacy

Securing real estate without money down is the first win. Sustaining it is where true ownership emerges. Anyone can structure one clever deal, but long-term wealth requires stability, management, and intention. Once you've activated your creative strategies, the next phase is about protecting your position, honoring your commitments, and transforming acquired properties into assets that serve purpose beyond profit. You didn't just come to play the game, you came to rewrite it for good.

Begin by fortifying what you've acquired. That means updating documents, recording deeds, reviewing contract timelines, and confirming every clause aligns with your current goals. No-money-down deals often have layered structures, seller agreements, wraparound financing, performance benchmarks, lease terms, so clarity is non-negotiable. You didn't pay upfront, which means your backend diligence must be airtight. If you're managing a subject-to property, confirm payment schedules and remain in constant communication. If you're executing a lease option, track every dollar invested in repairs so there's leverage when it's time to finalize the purchase.

Next, build operational systems. Ownership is more than holding a title, it's handling the weight. Who answers calls when repairs are needed? How do you screen tenants? How do you calculate cash flow without overlooking deferred maintenance or slow seasonal months? Investors who build portfolios without capital must double down on organization. That means software tools, trusted vendors, detailed ledgers, and proactive communication plans. You are not just protecting a house, you're managing a business rooted in vision and accountability.

Then, optimize the property to reinforce your financial elevation. Explore refinancing once value rises, positioning the asset to fund additional deals or secure reserves. Maximize rental income through upgrades that matter, curb appeal, insulation, safety features, not cosmetic hype. Consider equity partnerships for future acquisitions, using your first success as social proof. Because once you've succeeded without capital, your strategy becomes a magnet for others who want in. Don't waste that. Expand it wisely.

But the legacy-building part? That begins when your ownership impacts others. You offer young people a tour of the property, explaining the contract that made it possible. You write about the deal and share it with clarity so someone else in your position can try. You host meetups in the very property the bank said you couldn't afford. You're no longer just playing defense, you're teaching offense.

Ownership also means making values visible. If you're acquiring homes in vulnerable neighborhoods, make sure your approach reflects care, not conquest. Maintain your properties. Respect the culture. Hire locally. Offer mentorship. When you elevate a block, don't exploit it, empower it. No-money-down deals can be a tool for healing if the hands that close them are steady, honest, and informed by heart, not just profit.

This is where the movement sustains itself. You started with strategy. You now operate with stewardship. You turned limitation into leverage. You built something real from thin air and thick intention.

From here, ownership isn't about acquisition anymore, it's about preservation. It's about making sure what you build stands. It's about turning first deals into permanent impact.

CHAPTER FOUR

REHAB VS. ILLUSION: KNOWING THE REAL VALUE

Part One

"Pretty Paint" Doesn't Raise Value In A Dying Neighborhood

Every investor, homeowner, and real estate professional has heard it before: "It's move-in ready." "Completely rehabbed." "Fresh paint, new floors, updated fixtures." These are the buzzwords of surface-level renovation, phrases meant to attract attention, soften skepticism, and sell the illusion of improvement. But real value is never built in paint. And a dying neighborhood, no matter how glossy the interior of one home may be, cannot be revived by baseboards alone.

This chapter starts with hard truth: rehab can't hide environmental decline. You can install quartz countertops in a house surrounded by blight, and the property will still struggle to appreciate. You can refinish floors in a zip code plagued by crime, and buyers will still hesitate. You can stage a cozy living room in an area where public transportation has vanished, schools are underperforming, and every nearby business has boarded up and the open house will still feel empty. Because real estate is never just about what's inside the walls, it's about what's happening outside them.

Developers and wholesalers often prey on surface enthusiasm. They present properties with aesthetic upgrades, modern lighting, sleek bathroom tiling, freshly planted shrubs and market them as “hot buys.” But they avoid deeper questions. They won’t mention the abandoned structure next door. They won’t discuss the city’s lack of infrastructure investment. They won’t show the crime map or the vacancy rate. And if you’re not careful, you’ll believe the illusion. You’ll buy into curb appeal while ignoring the curb's reality.

This is why buyers, especially those investing with limited funds, must learn to separate cosmetic polish from neighborhood prognosis. That starts with walking the block before walking the house. You observe foot traffic, noise levels, litter patterns, lighting conditions, and overall energy. Is the street cared for? Are the nearby homes occupied and maintained? Is there police presence out of protection or escalation? Are children outside without fear, or does tension linger in every movement? If what you see beyond the property sends warning signals, the rehab inside may be nothing more than decoration in decline.

More importantly, real value is a product of sustainable safety, community function, and long-term potential. You assess not just the amenities inside a house, but the trajectory of the area. That means researching school performance. Pulling crime reports. Analyzing employment statistics. Reviewing city zoning plans. Speaking with local residents. If the neighborhood is shrinking, economically, emotionally, and structurally, your investment becomes hostage to that contraction. And no granite sink can change that.

To be clear: this isn’t a rejection of rehab. Thoughtful rehab in a rising or stabilizing community is an accelerator, it boosts appreciation, increases cash flow, and enhances livability. But rehab without surrounding health is lipstick on decay. It's a game of short-term optics with long-term loss. Buyers must train themselves to see through the shimmer. Because in real estate, illusion always costs more than inspection.

Part Two

Surroundings Define Worth—Community Health as Real Appraisal

Every property tells two stories: the one inside the walls and the one outside the windows. Investors who fail to understand this duality end up overpaying for cosmetic comfort in neighborhoods that offer no structural return. A house can gleam with renovations and sparkle with staging, but if the world around it is deteriorating, that glow fades fast. Real value is never built in isolation, it's built in relationship with its environment.

Start with infrastructure. Before you consider the square footage or the flooring finish, assess the city's investment in public systems. Are the roads well-maintained? Are storm drains functioning or flooded every time it rains? Is there public transit that links the neighborhood to opportunity, or do residents remain disconnected from work, school, and health care? Infrastructure is the skeleton of sustainable value. Without it, even the best rehabbed homes become traps for future loss.

Then, analyze school systems, not just their ratings, but their lived impact. Are students graduating? Are families engaged? Are schools under threat of closure or growing with momentum? A neighborhood's educational health signals everything about its direction. Even if you never plan to enroll a child, school performance influences resale value, rental demand, and long-term viability. A home two blocks from a collapsing school system will not appreciate simply because the cabinets are brand new.

Next, dive into commerce. Are local businesses active and thriving? Is the area littered with payday lenders and liquor stores, or does it feature grocery stores, cafes, clinics, and community centers? Healthy neighborhoods generate economic rhythm. If you invest in a property surrounded by boarded-up storefronts, you must either accept stagnation or commit to the work of revitalization. But know this: granite counters don't attract opportunity. Community function does.

Crime patterns matter just as much. Don't rely on hearsay or stereotypes, pull actual reports. Learn what types of incidents occur and how often. Are you seeing isolated events or patterns? Are residents organizing for safety? Is there visible prevention or reactive enforcement? A home may be priced attractively, but if residents fear walking outside after sunset, appreciation is compromised from the moment you sign.

This is not about perfection. Every community has its battles. It's about trajectory. Are the surroundings improving, fighting, rebuilding or collapsing? Your investment should align with your tolerance, your resources, and your principles. Buying in a challenged area requires a strategy that accounts for emotional, economic, and political forces, not just aesthetic potential.

Emotional geography plays a role too. Is the neighborhood proud? Do people speak with dignity and hope? Are porches active or silent? Are sidewalks cared for or overgrown? These cues inform the culture, rhythm, and promise embedded in the surroundings. And they determine whether your property is part of something growing or gasping.

Because ownership isn't just financial, it's relational. And until you've appraised the environment, you haven't truly appraised the home.

Part Three

Emotional Appraisal—Protect Your Family, Not Just the Property

Real estate is often described in numbers: square footage, comps, cap rates, and ROI. But beneath the math lies something more personal, more urgent: how the property makes your family feel, live, and grow. This emotional appraisal is rarely taught, almost never valued by professionals chasing percentages. Yet it's the foundation of generational protection. You're not just buying walls and wiring, you're investing in peace, safety, stability, and identity.

It starts with asking: Can your children walk down this street and feel safe? Not pretend safe. Not staged safe. Truly safe. Can elders sit on the porch without watching for chaos? Can teens bike home from school without crossing paths with trauma? These aren't sentimental questions, they're survival questions. Because no matter how pristine the rehab, if your loved ones cannot move freely in and around that property, the investment betrays its purpose.

When evaluating emotional worth, look at patterns, not just moments. One quiet afternoon doesn't erase years of tension. Talk to neighbors. Ask how things feel after sundown. Notice where people gather—or avoid. Check how often children play outside versus inside. If joy is missing from the rhythm of the community, your home's interior design means very little.

Emotional appraisal also includes psychological stamina. Will your family constantly be "on alert"? Is the neighborhood one argument away from eruption? Are there unresolved territorial tensions, overpolicing, or under-engagement from local leadership? These unseen forces drain the spirit and limit possibility. Buying a home in such a climate adds invisible tax to every experience, stress, anxiety, sleeplessness, and fear that undermines every "feature" of the property you paid for.

Think, too, about belonging. Do you feel welcome on this block? Are greetings exchanged, respect maintained, boundaries honored? Or is every glance a measurement of your legitimacy? A home that isolates your family socially is not a refuge, it's a prison with upgraded countertops. You need community flow, cultural harmony, and shared values. You need your children to grow without adapting to tension as normal.

And finally: consider the legacy you're building. Will your heirs inherit a space that nurtured them or one that hardened them? Will they remember this home as the place where you kept them safe or the place where they had to constantly survive? Emotional value cannot be overstated. It's the true appraisal, the one that shows up when the property's financial worth is irrelevant, and what's left is how it shaped lives.

Cosmetic upgrades may attract buyers, but emotional appraisal keeps families whole.

Part Four

Walk-Away Wisdom—When to Reject the Renovation Trap

One of the most essential traits of a strategic investor is discernment, the ability to see through polished presentations and ask, "Does this deal respect my future?" A house might dazzle with renovations, fresh paint, and updated features, but illusion often lives in the drywall. When surroundings scream decline and the community signals distress, walking away isn't failure, it's financial and emotional self-defense.

Cosmetic upgrades have become the bait in too many real estate traps. Developers stage properties to draw in desperate buyers, focusing on kitchen aesthetics and trendy bathroom remodels while ignoring the fact that the next block holds vacant lots, failing infrastructure, or toxic relationships with law enforcement. The property may be rehabbed, but if the environment is unstable, appreciation will stall and your peace will erode.

Buyers must learn the art of slowing down, not just to inspect the property, but to interrogate the context. That means pausing long enough to ask: Are community services present? Are schools thriving or threatened? Is transportation reliable or isolated? Are crime reports declining or escalating? What is the city's five-year development plan, and does this neighborhood exist within it or outside its concern?

Emotional pressure often clouds this judgment. The idea of finally "getting in the game" pushes buyers to accept rehabbed homes in compromised areas. Agents amplify that urgency. Friends cheer the deal. Families encourage the purchase. And suddenly the buyer feels guilty for considering a pause. But discernment must win over approval. There is no medal for buying a mistake and learning to endure it. There is only regret and the long-term strain of pretending it was worth it.

Walking away doesn't make you indecisive, it makes you aligned. You're stating clearly: I will not sacrifice safety for granite. I will not trade legacy for laminate. I will not bend my vision to fit a property that doesn't serve it. And when you step back from a deal, you signal not just discipline, but direction. You're choosing power over panic.

The investor who walks away from the wrong deal is the one best prepared to close the right one. That's the wisdom most never develop because they confuse momentum with progress. But progress requires alignment. And if the deal isn't aligned with your strategy, your spirit, and your standards, it's not your deal. No matter how pretty the walls are.

Part Five

The Investor's Blind Spot—The False Promise Of Quick Equity

Every buyer dreams of instant equity: the idea that a property can be rehabbed quickly, reappraised favorably, and either sold or rented for profit in weeks. It's a seductive vision, especially for new investors seeking fast validation and immediate returns. But beneath the fantasy lies a dangerous blind spot: the assumption that rehab equals value, and that upgrades alone can force the market to respond. In truth, unless those improvements are rooted in a healthy ecosystem, that equity is likely to be paper-thin or vanish altogether.

The real estate market doesn't reward effort, it rewards alignment. That means your rehab must align with the community's needs, the neighborhood's trajectory, and the buyer or tenant profile most likely to engage the area. You can add smart thermostats, luxury finishes, or even solar panels, but if the surrounding block communicates instability, your upgrades become irrelevant. Buyers won't overpay for fear. Renters won't stay long in discomfort. Appraisers won't ignore the gap between your renovations and the crime statistics two streets over.

Picture this: An investor puts $35,000 into a mid-century home, granite countertops, vinyl plank floors, fresh exterior paint, staged furniture, the works. On paper, it's a gem. But it's situated in a zip code with poor public transit, high property turnover, and stagnant school performance. The investor assumes the upgrades will justify a $60,000 increase in asking price. But the appraisal comes back just $15,000 above the original value. Why? Because the neighborhood metrics were never addressed. The market doesn't reward hope, it rewards context. And context was missing.

This is why investors must ground every rehab decision in external analysis. Before ordering materials or hiring contractors, pull comps across a half-mile radius. Map out infrastructure improvements or lack thereof. Speak with city planners if possible. Check upcoming zoning changes, neighborhood associations, or developer interest. If none exist, know that your rehab will have limited elevation power. You're building inside a vacuum. And vacuums aren't where wealth grows, they're where energy gets trapped.

What drives the blind spot is often pride. The desire to prove one's worth through transformation. The idea that a personal touch, an eye for design, or sweat equity can overcome all market conditions. It's noble, but dangerous. Because pride doesn't protect capital. Emotion doesn't shield families. A bold renovation in a deteriorating neighborhood might bring momentary satisfaction, but if the surroundings don't support sustainability, you're simply beautifying a struggle.

Instead, reframe your role. You're not just upgrading houses, you're evaluating ecosystems. You're deciding where effort translates to elevation, and where it becomes erasure. Sometimes the smartest move is pausing rehab until broader signals shift. Sometimes it's partnering with community leaders before picking a paint color. Sometimes it's choosing not to buy until you see health, not just hype.

Part Six

False Uplift—When Rehab Masks Community Neglect

There's a dangerous lie whispered in the real estate world: that a renovated property automatically means an improving neighborhood. It's a belief pushed by speculators, flippers, and agents desperate to trigger urgency. They point to stainless steel appliances, luxury flooring, and open-concept layouts as evidence of progress. But in many communities, these upgrades sit in isolation, cosmetic bandages applied to neighborhoods still bleeding from decades of neglect.

A rehabbed home in a neglected community doesn't change the schools, the policing, the infrastructure, or the economy. It doesn't erase the trauma from displacement or the absence of investment in local services. It doesn't rebuild bridges where trust has been broken between residents and the institutions that claim to serve them. And unless the rehab exists within a framework of sustained community uplift, it becomes a false beacon, bright but misleading.

This is where buyers must refuse to be seduced. You don't assess a property on its finishes, you assess it based on whether its existence contributes to equity or erasure. Who rehabbed it? Who will profit from the sale? Does this home exist in partnership with the block or in contrast to it? Are neighbors informed, involved, protected or are they being quietly priced out as these "new and improved" homes multiply? When rehab serves profit but disrespects proximity, it's an invasion, not an investment.

That's why buyers, especially those committed to legacy, must look beyond the drywall and into the story. A true investor doesn't just count bedrooms and bathrooms, they count community relationships, cultural integrity, and sustainability metrics. That means asking: Who lived here before? Why did they leave? Will your ownership stabilize or destabilize the area? Will your improvements attract authentic engagement or trigger speculative displacement?

And the key indicator in all of this is intention. Was the rehab done with care and knowledge of local history, or was it executed with speed for fast flipping? Are you being pitched a dream home, or a disguised asset meant to benefit someone far removed from the block?

Rehab must never be allowed to tell a lie. It must reflect truth, readiness, and respect. And if the house is beautiful but the community is being hollowed out to make room for outsiders with money and no mission, then the value is counterfeit. Ownership rooted in illusion always ends in erosion, of connection, of safety, of return.

Part Seven

When Developers Build Without Soul—Spotting Empty Upgrades

Modern real estate is full of spectacle, clean lines, glass finishes, neutral tones, and the ever-popular "open concept." Developers have figured out that if they standardize aesthetics and sprinkle in a few buzzwords, they can inflate value and shift attention away from deeper issues. They don't have to fix the block, the schools, or the public infrastructure. They just have to make the house look desirable enough to trigger emotional urgency. But beneath the shine, many of these homes are hollow, not in structure, but in spirit.

These upgrades are often formulaic. Walk into five newly rehabbed homes in struggling zip codes and you'll see the same flooring, the same recessed lighting, the same generic hardware. That's not investment, it's replication. And while some repetition is acceptable for scale, when developers build without responding to cultural identity, family function, or neighborhood resilience, they turn real estate into retail. The buyer walks out with keys, but no connection.

This is where soul matters. A home isn't just a place to sleep. It's where birthdays happen, where prayers are said, where traditions form, and futures are mapped. When developers treat neighborhoods like blank canvases for overpriced uniformity, they rob residents of context and memory. A rehab should respond to community, not erase it. If your home doesn't feel like part of the local story, it becomes an isolated pod, physically present but emotionally vacant.

Buyers need to look beyond "newness." Ask questions about the materials, the layout decisions, the energy efficiency, and the safety features. Were changes made to optimize the life of families, or just the optics of flipping? Is the design functional for elders, children, and working parents, or is it tailored for transient tenants looking for temporary style? Was the landscaping selected for local climate, sustainability, and privacy, or was it thrown in for photos?

Here's how you spot the difference: homes built with soul show intention in the details. They honor the rhythm of the street. Their design choices feel lived-in, not staged. They reflect care, not just calculation. And they respect the people, not just the market.

Ownership without soul invites alienation. Upgrades that ignore culture, connectivity, and collective memory create houses, not homes.

Part Eight

Manufactured Momentum—Recognizing Market Theater

In cities where reinvestment is trending and gentrification looms like a shadow, a new kind of illusion has emerged: manufactured momentum. This is the practice of using staged transactions, inflated comps, selective renovations, and curated media coverage to create the appearance of progress in areas that remain structurally unsupported. It's a theatrical version of economic development and buyers who fall for it risk anchoring their legacy in a neighborhood where the actors leave and the set collapses as soon as the camera pans away.

This illusion starts with selective rehab. A developer might renovate three properties on a block, install solar lights, plant new trees, and list each home at a price far above the historical average. Then, through internal transfers or investor coordination, they stage sales to set new comps. The listings close, the data hits public records, and the next wave of pricing climbs. But if you walk that block two months later, you'll notice the rest of the street untouched, still grappling with abandonment, underfunded schools, and unchecked crime. The "momentum" was a tactic, not a transformation.

Market theater also involves city narratives. Developers partner with local officials to promote future zoning changes, upcoming infrastructure improvements, or revitalization plans that sound promising but remain unfunded or delayed. Investors hear phrases like "emerging neighborhood" and "up-and-coming corridor" while real residents report no shifts in services or community health. The momentum feels exciting, but it's hollow. And buyers who depend on it to justify their purchase often discover they were sold anticipation, not reality.

Buyers must develop tools to cut through this fog. Start by mapping actual progress, not proposed plans. Pull permit data. Track which infrastructure projects have broken ground and which remain in discussion. Review school district budgets and recent performance scores, not just talk of charter openings. Study whether businesses are entering and thriving or leaving quietly under lease strain. Local newspapers and online listings tell one story, but walking the neighborhood and speaking to residents tells the truth.

Also pay attention to who's being centered. If every property pitch spotlights "young professionals" and "investor-friendly opportunities," but fails to mention the actual demographics of the block, you're not being told a growth story, you're being sold a displacement model. Real progress includes integration, opportunity, and preservation. Momentum that only benefits outsiders is exploitation dressed up as urban renewal.

As an investor, your job isn't just to participate, it's to protect. You must ask: Is this rehab part of a real shift or an isolated spark? Am I aligning with movement or marketing? Will this investment support community growth or destabilize it further?

Because when you buy into theater, you inherit its expiration date. Real value comes from reality, not performance.

Final Part

Anchoring Ownership In Truth—Beyond Renovation, Toward Restoration

There comes a moment when every buyer, builder, and investor must confront the deeper question: Is this property rooted in truth or temptation? Because rehab can seduce. It can mask systemic wounds, silence legitimate fears, and paint over histories that demand acknowledgment. But if your ownership journey is to last, if the legacy you build is meant to stand, it must be anchored in truth, not trend.

Truth begins with transparency. That means refusing to ignore the story of the land you're buying. It means researching who lived there before, how the neighborhood shifted, whether displacement played a role in the current market opportunity. It means recognizing that every home sits inside a larger web, of economics, of policy, of social rhythm and if your purchase contributes to erasure rather than elevation, your renovation means nothing.

Buyers must evolve beyond aesthetic checklisting. You don't walk into a home looking only for open layouts and marble counters. You listen for silence in the streets, check the pulse of local businesses, feel the rhythm of real lives, not just the curated experience offered during a showing. You make decisions not just based on what pleases the eye, but on what aligns with your values.

Restoration is the next chapter of ownership. It goes further than rehab. It respects context, honors culture, and invests in community continuity. That might mean hiring local contractors. Building relationships with neighbors.

Supporting block associations. Partnering with schools. It means treating your acquisition as a bridge, not a barricade. You become a steward, not just a resident.

And for investors, restoration means responsible development. You evaluate whether your profit model amplifies displacement or invites dignity. You prioritize long-term relationships over short-term margins. You build portfolios that reflect not just financial intelligence, but emotional awareness. Because if your gains come from someone else's loss, you haven't elevated, you've extracted.

Real value in real estate lives at the intersection of equity, integrity, and vision. It's not found in the tile. It's found in the truth. And when you build from that foundation, every purchase, every rehab, every rental or resale becomes more than a transaction. It becomes testimony.

CHAPTER FIVE

NEIGHBORHOODS LIE—LEARN TO READ BETWEEN THE LINES

Part One

The Illusion Of Price—Why Asking Means Nothing Without Context

In the world of real estate, price is often treated like gospel. A seller lists a home for $265,000, and agents frame it as a deal, investors call it promising, and buyers start stretching budgets to make it fit. But here's the truth that most professionals won't say out loud: asking price is marketing. It's not a reflection of real value, it's a projection, a tactic, and at times, a trap. To treat asking price as truth is to enter a negotiation already manipulated.

Let's dissect what price really represents. On paper, it's supposed to reflect the property's market worth based on size, location, condition, and comparable sales. But in practice, price is shaped by urgency, speculation, hype, and psychological strategy. Sellers inflate numbers based on emotion or perceived renovations. Agents suggest price points to test the waters, stimulate bidding wars, or push neighborhoods into new valuation tiers. Flippers price for profit, not fairness. And developers often insert premiums based on upcoming city initiatives that haven't even broken ground. So when a property hits the market, the number you see is rarely neutral, it's engineered.

That's why context must be your first layer of protection. Without it, the price becomes a weapon against your ignorance. Start by pulling comps, but don't just compare square footage and bedroom count. Examine when those comps sold, under what conditions, and whether they included seller concessions or post-sale price adjustments. A home selling for $240,000 after sitting 90 days isn't proof the block supports that value, it's proof someone accepted a number, possibly under pressure or manipulated expectation.

Next, look at time-on-market trends. If homes in the area are listed for 30 days but closing in 120, price is being rejected by buyers silently. Sellers list high, but negotiations keep pulling value lower. That gap between list price and final sale price is crucial, because it shows where truth lives. And yet many agents only show you the asking numbers, hoping you won't investigate what actually stuck.

Neighborhood trajectory also matters. Is the area appreciating based on real development or just speculative buzz? New coffee shops don't mean new infrastructure. Staged community events don't mean systemic change. A few painted facades on a decaying street mean little unless the city, residents, and businesses commit to long-term action. If prices are rising faster than local employment, education, or safety metrics, you're watching a bubble,not progress.

Buyers must question the logic behind every number. Who set the price, and why? What assumptions were baked into it? Was it based on nearby gentrification trends, or was it inflated to bait buyers desperate to avoid another bidding war? Agents often say, "It's priced to sell," but that's shorthand for "priced for emotion." Smart investors respond not with excitement, but with excavation.

Consider the renovation factor. A rehabbed home may justify a price increase, but only if the rehab matches structural need and neighborhood momentum. If the seller added granite countertops and recessed lighting but ignored foundational damage, old wiring, or bad plumbing, the price is inflated based on appearance. That's economic illusion wrapped in cosmetic convenience. Buyers must dissect what was upgraded, what was ignored, and how those decisions reflect or distort the true value of the property in its context.

Also, interrogate the selling strategy. Is the home being pitched with urgency? "Will go fast." "Multiple offers already in." "Owner motivated." These phrases are designed to heighten anxiety and trigger emotional commitment before logic can intervene. But remember: urgency is manufactured. If the home is truly valuable, it will stand without theatrics. If it's overhyped, the noise is hiding a deeper problem.

Then there's appraisal manipulation. Sellers or their agents may point to recent appraisals to validate price, but who paid for the appraisal? Was it challenged? Did it factor in all environmental risks or just internal upgrades? Many appraisals lean conservative unless pushed, and even then, they reflect snapshot judgment, not long-term wisdom. Smart buyers supplement formal appraisals with community research, historical pricing maps, and an understanding of investment risk based on nearby developments or lack thereof.

The most important tool in this process is clarity. Clarity cancels out suggestion. It says, "I see your price, and I understand your motive." It allows you to separate emotional bait from strategic value. And it arms you to enter negotiation with confidence, not desperation.

When you understand that price is part of the performance, not the truth, you stop reacting and start analyzing. You refuse to overpay for hype. You refuse to compete for illusion. You commit to ownership that honors context, not just cost. Because real wealth isn't built through acceptance, it's built through interrogation.

Part Two

Beneath The Surface—When Drug Zones, Abandoned Lots, And Broken Systems Hide Behind Renovation

The freshly painted porch. The stylish mailbox. The new roofline that gleams under morning light. To the casual observer, the house looks perfect, reborn even. A symbol of growth. But five steps beyond the lot line, you see it: an abandoned building with boards nailed so tight they hide decades of decay. A corner where young men gather, watching every vehicle with intensity. A store nearby that closes early, not because of inventory, but safety. You're not looking at a neighborhood in transition, you're looking at a neighborhood hiding its truth. And unless you know how to read the patterns beneath the polish, you'll buy into illusion disguised as opportunity.

Real estate deception doesn't start with fraud, it starts with omission. Agents highlight curb appeal and cosmetic upgrades, but rarely discuss the social dynamics that shape value long after the keys are handed over. Renovation becomes the camouflage. Investors flood areas with quick flips and prefab upgrades that mask broken systems beneath the drywall. Buyers who aren't trained to question environment over aesthetics find themselves owning homes surrounded by neglect, dysfunction, or unspoken danger.

Drug zones are the first layer of this complexity. They're rarely listed on property descriptions and often dismissed as "improving areas," but their impact is real, economically, emotionally, and structurally. A block with active narcotics trafficking shifts the rhythm of life. Residents adjust routines to avoid confrontation. Children learn shortcuts to school not because they're efficient, but because they're safer. Nighttime becomes tactical. And even with renovation surrounding the corner, buyers will struggle to retain tenants, grow equity, or feel secure in their investment.

This presence affects more than safety, it affects perception. Lenders, appraisers, and insurers often calculate risk based on local crime data and law enforcement patterns. If your rehabbed home sits adjacent to a known trafficking corridor, your valuation shrinks, premiums rise, and financing options constrict. These effects don't show up on the for-sale flyer or in the listing photos, but they arrive the moment you take possession. Unless you did the homework, you'll inherit problems disguised as potential.

Then there's abandonment, lots left to rot, buildings half-demolished, homes with no clear title or ownership. These spaces are the silent leak in every real estate deal. On paper, they may be listed as future development sites or "opportunity zones." But their presence signals disconnection. No matter how beautiful your property is, abandoned lots nearby communicate abandonment of care, of investment, of sustained commitment. And buyers cannot build long-term equity next to silence.

You must ask: Who's responsible for these lots? Has the city prioritized redevelopment or simply documented decline? Are there active community plans to reintegrate abandoned spaces into housing, green zones, or commerce or are they simply tolerated as part of local decay? If the surrounding environment lacks momentum, your home becomes an island, one with eroding shores.

Even more insidious are broken systems that lie underneath: failing school districts, unreliable utilities, strained health services, understaffed emergency response, and disconnected governance. These systems determine whether your property supports life or stifles it. A newly renovated home means nothing if the school next door hasn't seen textbooks updated in ten years. It means less if the nearest hospital is chronically understaffed, or if rolling blackouts are part of the city's seasonal "plan."

Buyers often don't investigate these systems until they're already burdened by them. The excitement of purchase overshadows the interrogation of service. But real ownership requires proactive awareness. Before you buy, you research the funding history of local schools. You review utility performance reports. You speak with block captains, ward representatives, and community leaders. You walk the neighborhood twice: once during the day, and once at night. You attend local meetings, even virtually. If what you find is dysfunction in disguise, you reconsider. Because no matter how sleek the cabinets are, they cannot clean the water if the system fails.

So why don't agents disclose these truths upfront? Because market illusion is profitable. When neighborhoods are dressed up with rehabbed properties but lack supporting infrastructure, it allows sellers to benefit from asymmetry, knowledge they hold, and problems buyers haven't been taught to detect. It's not always malicious, but it is manipulative. And unless you learn to reverse engineer the neighborhood's story, you'll fall victim to packaging that masks pain.

The solution is rooted in rhythm. Good neighborhoods have rhythms of growth, visible in everyday life. You see multiple generations coexisting. You see local businesses building relationship, not just revenue. You see porch culture, residents outside, talking, exchanging. You see participation in politics, in schools, in block planning. You see police presence grounded in service, not intimidation. If the rhythm is broken, sporadic movement, constant vacancy, visible tension, then the renovation you're buying is a staged scene, not a sustainable investment.

Negotiation also requires awareness. If you recognize that a property sits inside a challenged ecosystem, you adjust your terms accordingly. You request seller concessions. You demand detailed documentation of repairs and warranties. You lower your price ceiling because context limits upside. You negotiate from truth, not optimism.

And you prepare exit strategies. If you're buying with the intention to renovate and rent, have contingency plans for vacancy or pricing adjustment. If you're planning to live in the home, understand what advocacy will be required post-purchase to improve the surrounding environment. Know what allies exist. Know what plans are underway. If none of that is available, ask yourself: Are you ready to be the only investment surrounded by neglect?

Ultimately, real estate is never about the property alone. It's about the system that surrounds it, sustains it, or suffocates it. Buyers must learn to read between the listings, beneath the upgrades, and around the corner, iterally. You walk the alley. You speak to the store clerk. You count active homes. You observe energy. Because the real story of any neighborhood lives in its patterns—not its presentation.

Rehab without realism is a trap. Ownership without awareness is a lie. And if your purchase doesn't honor the full truth of the environment, it's not a legacy—it's a liability dressed up as a dream.

Part Three

Seeing the Signals—Spotting Red Flags and Negotiating What's Fair

There's a quiet language neighborhoods speak and unless you know how to interpret it, you'll buy into a lie. Every street has signals. Every block communicates its health, rhythm, and risk long before you step inside a showing. It's not about paranoia, it's about pattern recognition. Because when sellers inflate price, agents decorate dysfunction, and developers stage renaissance where none exists, the only protection buyers have is their ability to read between the lines and negotiate from truth, not illusion.

Start with physical indicators. These red flags rarely appear in listings but shout their presence to anyone paying attention. Look at how sidewalks are maintained. Are they cracked, overgrown, full of litter? Healthy neighborhoods typically reflect collective care, even when funds are limited. If city crews haven't serviced sidewalks in years, that signals disinvestment. Look at porch activity. Are residents sitting outside, greeting each other, walking dogs, managing kids? Or is there silence, tension, boarded windows, and minimal interaction? Presence reveals culture. Absence reveals instability.

Don't forget lighting. Streetlights that flicker or remain broken for weeks suggest neglect, not just by residents, but by infrastructure systems designed to maintain safety. Do you see security bars on every window? Multiple warning signs posted on fences? These may reflect past trauma and may forecast future disruption. It's not about judging, it's about decoding. A rehabbed home surrounded by warning signs is like a luxury car parked in a flood zone. Looks good, but not designed to last where it sits.

Now go deeper. Speak to people, not just agents. Visit nearby stores and ask how business has been. Chat with neighbors on the block, not just the ones cherry-picked to give glowing reviews. Ask direct questions: "How long have you lived here?" "Have things improved in recent years?" "Do families feel safe walking at night?" The answers won't always be clean, but they will be honest. And if you hear stories of turnover, eviction, tension with law enforcement, or community conflict, recognize that you're not just buying a house, you're stepping into a storm.

Vacant homes and lots should never be ignored. They tell stories that renovation cannot rewrite. Was the block once thriving and now quiet? Are those vacancies seasonal or structural? Are they tied to systemic abandonment or personal hardship? Too many investors overlook empty lots as potential future builds. But sometimes, those lots are symbols of unresolved trauma, foreclosures, failed projects, legal entanglements. And your investment may inherit the shadows cast by those histories.

School quality is another red flag and one of the most ignored. Buyers who don't have children often dismiss the issue entirely. But school district health directly impacts property value, tenant retention, and resale potential. Review test scores. Graduation rates. Funding patterns. Teacher turnover. Community involvement. If nearby schools are underfunded or suffering administrative collapse, buyers must factor that into their valuation model. Because homeownership isn't just about today, it's about tomorrow. And tomorrow depends on education.

Public transit access matters too. If the property sits in a so-called "emerging neighborhood" but lacks reliable connections to job centers, medical services, or cultural hubs, its value will plateau. Rehab doesn't mean integration. You must assess connectivity. Are residents reliant on vehicles? Is the area walkable? Are buses consistent, and does the city have plans for transit expansion? A home isolated from opportunity, even if rehabbed, becomes a beautiful cage.

Now let's talk police patterns. Law enforcement visibility isn't always about protection. In some neighborhoods, it signals control, tension, or unresolved conflict. Pull actual crime data, not just generic summaries. Is the area plagued by property crimes, assaults, drug activity, or civil unrest? Are crimes increasing or stabilizing? Does the presence of law enforcement stem from collaboration or confrontation?

Ask these questions without fear. Ownership requires courage.

And then there are emotional flags, the ones harder to name, but impossible to ignore. Does the energy of the block feel tense or toxic? Are there frequent loud confrontations, visible stress signals, or quiet avoidance in public space? Do families seem to adapt their routines to avoid danger or do they flow freely across space and time? These emotional undercurrents often mean more than any renovation or market indicator. Because a house wrapped in tension will never feel like home, no matter what the staging says.

Once you've spotted the red flags, the next step is negotiation. This doesn't mean bargaining blindly, it means presenting data, context, and clarity to justify a fair price. If comps are inflated based on staged sales, you challenge them with deeper analysis. If the rehab ignored foundational issues or the block remains unstable, you lower your offer to match real value, not perceived hype. If you detect risk, structural, social, or systemic, you ask for seller concessions. You request extended inspection timelines. You demand transparency. Because negotiation rooted in truth builds confidence and protects your future.

Use language that anchors your analysis. Say, "Based on local school ratings, crime data, and vacancy patterns, this home does not justify the current asking price." Say, "The renovations are noted, but given the surrounding disinvestment and limited public services, we'd need an adjustment to proceed." Say, "We've researched upcoming zoning plans and found no confirmed development within five blocks, our offer reflects that reality." These statements are not combative, they are corrective. They signal intelligence. And sellers often respond with respect when buyers show rigor.

You also negotiate emotionally. If you're living in the home, remind agents and sellers that your concern includes safety, community, and long-term stability, not just decor. That kind of honesty reframes you from amateur buyer to strategic steward. You're not just walking into a property, you're walking into history. And unless the price respects both, you walk away without apology.

Because here's the truth: Red flags aren't deal breakers. But they are deal definers. And when you see them clearly, you build deals not on dreams, but on depth.

Final Part

Unmasking Value—From Inflation To Negotiation Power

At the end of every property tour, there's a moment, a quiet pause when the buyer asks themselves: Is this worth it? Not based on what the agent said. Not based on how fresh the paint smells or how well the kitchen was staged. But based on what's not being said. Based on what the block didn't show. Based on what the data whispered and what the neighborhood tried to distract you from. Because beneath every asking price, there's a game and smart buyers know how to rewrite the rules.

Real estate inflation isn't always caused by greed. Sometimes, it's driven by desperation. Sellers overprice because they're chasing past equity that's already evaporated. Developers inflate because they've spent more on quick flips than the market can reasonably sustain.

Agents push numbers to meet commission goals. And in neighborhoods touched by early gentrification, asking prices often reflect a fantasy version of value, a version that anticipates what a block could become, not what it currently is. You must learn to spot that fantasy and reject it when it doesn't honor reality.

Begin with appraisal trends. Pull reports on similar properties sold in the last six months, not just within a one-mile radius, but within a cultural radius. Did those homes reflect real neighborhood momentum, or were they isolated rehabs in struggling blocks? Were buyers local or out-of-town speculators? Was the average closing price dropping or rising? And most importantly: what are homes actually selling for versus what they're being listed at? That ratio reveals truth. If homes are listed at $300,000 but consistently closing around $245,000, you have leverage.

Next, use behavioral analysis. How long has the property been listed? Has the asking price changed? Have showings increased or plateaued? Does the listing say "motivated seller"? Are there open houses every weekend without contracts on the table? These are signs of inflation without traction, offers rejected, reality resisted, and a seller holding on to a price that the market no longer supports. That's your opening.

Layer in environmental context. Look at zoning maps, infrastructure investment, public records, and civic plans. If the neighborhood has not received recent funding for schools, parks, roads, or transit, its "hot" designation may be purely speculative. If surrounding businesses are operating with reduced hours, reporting theft or vandalism, or failing to hire locally, the ecosystem is fractured. You negotiate from that fracture. You present facts, not feelings.

Now enter negotiation mode, not as a hopeful buyer, but as an educated strategist.

Your language must be precise. Say, "Based on documented school performance, crime index fluctuations, and current lending restrictions for this zip code, the asking price exceeds what this block can sustain." Say, "Although the renovation is appreciated, analysis of surrounding vacancy rates and abandonment history suggests this home should be valued 12–18% lower than currently listed." Say, "We've reviewed nearby comps and accounting for economic stagnation in the region, our offer reflects grounded equity, not inflated hype."

These aren't just negotiation tactics, they're declarations of understanding. They show sellers you've done the work. You're not reacting to pretty cabinets, you're responding to structural truth.

Also, never negotiate in isolation. Bring documentation. Assemble a mini dossier: crime maps, school funding charts, property tax increases, infrastructure reports, even environmental hazard data if applicable. Sellers and agents expect emotion, they are disarmed by information. When you show up with evidence, you're not just buying a house, you're auditing a system.

And here's the real leverage: silence.

Don't rush your offer. Let your review period breathe. Ask for time to walk the block at different hours. Speak with nearby property managers. Review eviction filings in the neighborhood. Sellers fear silent buyers because silence means thought. When you delay unnecessarily, you lose credibility. But when you delay strategically, you gain power.

For legacy buyers, those purchasing to build generational wealth, the negotiation must also honor future impact. Frame your offer not just as financial, but principled. Say, "We intend to protect and uplift this neighborhood through local hiring, property stewardship, and community engagement. We are committed to more than profit. But our offer reflects both that commitment and the structural challenges surrounding this home."

This level of language shifts the energy. Sellers stop seeing you as a lowballer, they start seeing you as a stabilizer. And they are more likely to work with stabilizers than speculators, especially if the home has emotional or historical significance.

Also, insert guardrails. If you agree to price terms near inflation levels, request protections: post-sale inspection clauses, renovation guarantees, contractor warranties. Negotiate escrow arrangements that allow for review. Build in contingencies based on environmental assessments or community feedback. You are not just protecting your money, you're protecting your peace.

And never forget: walking away is negotiation. Every "no" you deliver echoes beyond that deal. It sets standards. Agents remember. Sellers remember. Your reputation builds. And in markets full of fluff and fantasy, a buyer known for clarity becomes a magnet for real opportunity.

Because in truth, most people don't negotiate, they accept.

They accept that asking price equals worth.

They accept that a granite kitchen justifies gentrification.

They accept that a staged home in a broken block is still a blessing.

You are not most people. You interrogate systems. You challenge presentations. You strip illusion until only truth remains.

And when you do that, you never overpay, not just in dollars, but in dignity.

CHAPTER SIX

THE APPRAISAL TRUTH: VALUE ISN'T ALWAYS VISIBLE

Part One

Seeing Through The Surface—Redefining What Makes A Home Valuable

In the real estate industry, value is often defined by metrics. A home's worth is calculated based on market comps, square footage, lot size, materials used, upgrades completed, and proximity to high-demand zones. It's a transactional process, carried out by appraisers trained to assign numbers to spaces regardless of the lives held within them. But for buyers who move with strategy and soul, this system falls short. Because true value is not just visible, it is lived, felt, and experienced. It moves beyond market data and reaches into the heartbeat of a community.

Market comps can tell you what other homes have sold for. They can offer snapshots of nearby prices and suggest trends in appreciation. But they cannot tell you if the block feels safe after dark. They cannot measure the trust between neighbors or the warmth of a community where children play outside without fear. They don't account for local mentorship programs, Black-owned businesses providing jobs, or residents organizing to repair the infrastructure when the city ignores their calls. Comps miss culture. They miss context. They cannot appraise dignity.

That's why buyers must develop their own valuation systems, models that honor not just property, but people. Begin by identifying the social indicators. What is the rhythm of the neighborhood? Is there active community engagement? Do residents attend school board meetings, fight for clean water, advocate for better policing, and celebrate each other's milestones? Are the sidewalks cared for, not just by city workers but by those who live there? These signs signal investment, not of money, but of meaning. A block where people are emotionally invested is a block that resists decay.

Safety is another pillar. Traditional appraisal systems may factor in crime data but often fail to interrogate how safety feels. Buyers must walk the block, engage with residents, and observe behaviors. Do families stroll without looking over their shoulders? Are parks full during daylight hours and silent at night? Does law enforcement engage responsibly or reactively? Are elders visible, cared for, and protected? A safe community supports mental peace, physical well-being, and generational stability. And no granite countertop can replace that peace once violated.

Schools, too, carry immense weight, far beyond test scores. Yes, you must check academic performance, funding levels, and graduation rates. But dig deeper. Are students treated with care? Are teachers equipped and supported? Is the school culturally relevant, inclusive, and engaged with families? Does it reflect the block's values or attempt to override them with external systems? A strong school isn't just a selling point, it's a pillar of development, creating pathways for children to learn with pride and prepare with power. Buying near a school committed to equity and excellence is a strategy for legacy, not just resale.

And while these social metrics matter, stability binds them together. A neighborhood in flux, displaced by speculation or slowly hollowed out, cannot offer sustained value. Buyers must look at how long residents stay, how often properties turn over, and whether generational continuity exists. Are grandparents, parents, and children living nearby or scattered due to unaffordable pricing and eviction trends? Are cultural institutions present and protected? If not, the house may rise in price, but fall in purpose.

Now shift into emotional appraisal. What does it feel like to stand on the porch and breathe? Does your body tense or release? Are you greeted or ignored? Do your children smile or shrink when walking the sidewalk? These reactions matter. Buyers often downplay emotional intelligence in favor of financial calculation, only to discover too late that fear has no refund policy. Buying into a neighborhood where your family feels invisible, unsafe, or unwelcome is not ownership, it is exile.

Community awareness plays a role here. When evaluating a home, ask about its history. Who lived here before? What was their story? Was their exit peaceful or pressured? Was the home part of cultural movement, migration patterns, or resistance? Have developers tried to erase its legacy? Is the property being flipped for profit without regard for the neighborhood's heart? Buyers must resist participating in that erasure. You don't just buy four walls, you inherit a narrative. Your presence should restore, not erase.

To appraise with dignity means creating a valuation that honors the family entering the home. Ask if the space allows each member to thrive. Is there room for elders to age comfortably? Are there quiet areas for studying, safe areas for children to play, and gathering spaces for celebration? Is the layout conducive to spiritual practice, cultural rituals, rest, nourishment, and creativity? Every property has a purpose and buyers must decide if that purpose aligns with their mission.

Buyers must also assess whether their presence benefits or disrupts the community. If your purchase contributes to displacement, silence, or fear, the property may be beautiful, but the ownership is broken. You must ask if your financial model includes respect. Will you hire locally? Support nearby businesses? Engage respectfully with traditions and customs? Share your resources? Uplift the block through partnership, not just presence?

And then comes the final layer: future potential. What can be built from this home, not just profit, but possibility? Can your child launch a dream here? Can elders pass down wisdom? Can you host workshops, feed neighbors, mentor youth, and grow with grace? Is this home a container for your legacy, or simply a shell for your belongings? Value lives in vision. And if your purchase aligns with the future you intend to build, then it is truly worthy, regardless of what the spreadsheet says.

Traditional appraisals serve a purpose. They inform lenders, establish tax benchmarks, and protect institutions. But as a buyer moving with purpose, you must build an appraisal rooted in soul, strategy, and stewardship. You must learn to see value not just in features, but in futures.

Part Two

Building A Human-Centered Appraisal Model

When you strip away the spreadsheets and sales tactics, when you move past the market cycles and polished presentations, what's left is the question that most buyers never get taught to ask: Does this space honor the lives it will hold? That question lives at the center of human-centered appraisal, a model of property evaluation that resists commodification and refocuses attention on dignity, family preservation, cultural resonance, and communal alignment. It's not that math doesn't matter, it's that meaning matters more.

To build this model, begin by rethinking value itself. Value isn't just worth, it's welcome. A home becomes valuable when it receives its residents with grace, protects them without condition, and allows them to evolve without apology. This means your appraisal system must account for emotional fit, community rhythm, spatial function, and cultural integrity. It's a blend of social science, intuition, and strategic realism, one capable of filtering through neighborhood mythology to land on truth.

Start with emotional fit. Does the architecture feel like a home or a product? Are the ceilings low and suppressive, or open and encouraging? Do windows offer light and connection, or expose vulnerability and surveillance? Is the layout built to contain joy, movement, rest, and restoration, or does it merely replicate whatever was popular in flipped homes last year? Many buyers settle for structure because they've been conditioned to see shelter as success. But shelter without spirit becomes confinement. Your appraisal must interrogate whether the physical container of the home expands your family's ability to feel and flourish.

Next is community rhythm. Does the block breathe in sync with your values? Are mornings full of warmth, neighbors waving, children walking with rhythm, elders greeting the day? Are weekends active with collaboration, service, or celebration or are they tense, quiet, or forced? Do people move with ownership or avoidance? A valuable home isn't just about what you see inside, it's about what you feel when you stand outside and realize your name, your face, your future belongs here.

Functional design comes into play too. Does the space actually serve the day-to-day needs of those who'll live there? Is there room for generational layering, where grandparents, children, and grandchildren can coexist without friction? Are kitchens designed for real cooking, not just visual appeal? Are bedrooms soundproofed enough for rest? Are bathrooms accessible for elders with mobility challenges? Are there spaces for solitude and spaces for gathering? A functional home is more than photogenic, it's durable across seasons of life.

Cultural integrity adds another dimension. Does the home allow you to practice your traditions? Can you honor rituals without rearranging the entire layout? Is there space for prayer, storytelling, art, music, rest, grief, and renewal? Will the structure amplify your identity or ask you to mute it to conform with an aesthetic you never chose? Buyers must ask themselves not just how the home looks, but how it listens. If the home cannot hold your history, it cannot support your future.

Beyond the property, the human-centered appraisal model expands to encompass social health. A valuable neighborhood is one where institutions work toward justice, not just function. This means reviewing the local ecosystem: Are clinics accessible? Are teachers supported? Are libraries funded? Are community gardens active? Are young people offered leadership opportunities? Are elders honored? Are streets built for walking, gathering, and sharing? These aren't decorative questions, they're structural. A neighborhood that isolates its residents, dismisses their needs, or erases their heritage cannot support wealth, not financial, emotional, or spiritual.

The human-centered model also adjusts for trauma. If the area was previously redlined, over-policed, disinvested, or exploited, then renovation doesn't equal restoration. Buyers must research the arc of the block, not just the last ten years, but the last forty. Who left, who stayed, who was forced out? What languages were spoken here? What music, food, rituals, and resistance lived here? Did the city build walls or bridges? Did developers bring people together or silence them with profit? A buyer rooted in legacy cannot purchase without unpacking this context. Because ownership, when done right, redeems space, it doesn't erase it.

Preservation plays a critical role. A valuable home is one you can protect, not just from weather, but from erasure. That means understanding deed restrictions, zoning protections, and neighborhood organizing efforts. Can you remodel responsibly? Can you share your space with community initiatives? Can you convert unused areas into micro-libraries, mentorship rooms, or garden plots? Does the property allow innovation without violating tradition?

Human-centered appraisal asks: Not just can I live here, but can I serve here, sustain here, and leave something behind?

Now turn inward. Appraise yourself. Will living here honor your health, mental, physical, and spiritual? Will it energize you, stabilize you, and elevate your relationships? Will your children gain clarity and courage or confusion and compromise? Will you be seen, not just as a homeowner, but as a human? Because value isn't a number, it's a naming. When you walk in and feel yourself fully present, fully allowed, fully capable of creating something real, you've found more than a property, you've found possibility.

Lastly, human-centered appraisal includes responsibility. If the home you're buying pushes someone else out, inflates rental prices, or disturbs long-standing community rhythms, then the value is one-sided. You gain, but someone else loses. This must be addressed. Consider ownership models that include community preservation clauses. Research land trusts, cooperative housing approaches, shared investment systems. Ask whether your purchase fits into a larger ecosystem or whether it disrupts it. Value must be mutual.

This model isn't common, but it's necessary. Because the old way of valuing homes, through comps, cosmetics, and speculative pricing, has bred exclusion, trauma, and theft. Human-centered appraisal restores balance. It allows buyers to hold both power and accountability. It means the home you buy doesn't just shine, it serves.

Part Three

Preserving Legacy—Appraisal As A Tool For Family Continuity And Community Strength

For many families, especially those building generational wealth against a backdrop of historical exclusion, homeownership isn't just a financial milestone, it's a declaration. It says, "We belong here. We will not be moved. We will build and keep building." But if the criteria used to acquire that home fails to center family preservation, community alignment, and cultural longevity, the asset may end up eroding what it was meant to protect. That's why appraisal, when done with intention, becomes more than a numeric judgment, it becomes a tool of continuity.

Preserving legacy begins with redefining what the home holds. It's not just shelter, it's memory. It carries the laughter of children discovering themselves, the tears of elders recounting histories, the prayers whispered over meals and milestones. And when families treat their living space as a repository of purpose, not just possession, the structure becomes sacred. The walls stop being barriers and start becoming bridges, tying generations together through shared rhythm, responsibility, and ritual.

Appraising with this mindset starts by assessing the space for multigenerational fluidity. Can elders live comfortably without stairs or constant assistance? Are there quiet zones for study, creative expression, or spiritual practice? Can the home flex in times of crisis, like taking in relatives, hosting community meetings, or responding to health challenges? These qualities don't show up in traditional evaluations, but they determine whether the home uplifts or constrains.

Spatial dignity is critical here. Does the home offer privacy and proximity? Can conversations happen without interruption? Can family members retreat for self-care without isolating from connection? Are there spaces designed for play, healing, growth, and intergenerational dialogue? A home without these affordances may be priced high, but its internal value is low. Because legacy isn't built on transaction, it's built on transformation.

The neighborhood's role in legacy cannot be overstated. A home surrounded by instability, disinvestment, or silent hostility becomes a site of tension, not continuity. Buyers must evaluate whether the block allows generational identity to flourish. Are cultural practices welcomed or silenced? Are young people mentored or monitored? Are elders respected or ignored? These factors shape whether the family grows together or fractures under environmental stress.

Community reciprocity also defines value. A home becomes more valuable when it connects the family to others, neighbors, business owners, organizers, educators, spiritual leaders. These ties create resilience. They allow legacy to expand beyond the individual household into collective movement. When buyers choose homes in neighborhoods aligned with their vision, they build protective ecosystems, not just portfolios.

Appraisal, in this context, includes impact forecasting. Ask yourself: If my family stays here for ten years, what will we gain? What will we risk? Will this home allow my children to root their identities or force them to adapt to spaces not built for them? Will I be forced to explain, again and again, why our culture matters? Will we be treated as guests or as generational pillars?

Financial metrics come last, but they still matter. Legacy requires sustainability. That means reviewing taxes, insurance trends, refinancing opportunities, and equity growth. But don't view these in isolation. Ask whether the financial structure of the deal protects your family or exposes them to future instability. Are monthly costs predictable and manageable across life stages? Can renovations be done without sacrificing essentials? Can the property be passed down without triggering burdensome capital gains or title confusion?

Buyers committed to legacy must also assess repairability. If something breaks, physically or socially, can it be fixed with dignity? Are contractors accessible and fair? Is there a network of service providers who honor community values? If your roof leaks, do you have support nearby or are you left dealing with overpriced corporations who treat you as a transaction? A valuable home offers local healing, not distant service.

Family preservation includes psychological safety. Ask not just about crime rates, but emotional climate. Will your children feel pride or pressure? Will they speak their truth without fearing contradiction? Will their bodies, minds, and spirits remain intact across years of exposure to the neighborhood's rhythm? These aren't rhetorical questions, they're blueprints. And homes that compromise emotional health undermine legacy, no matter how elegant the interior design.

Community awareness must extend into collaboration. When you appraise a home, consider how your family's presence can contribute. Can your elders offer wisdom to the block? Can your children engage with local youth organizations? Can your household support initiatives like voter registration drives, block cleanups, or holiday gatherings? If the property isolates you from others, it limits your potential for legacy-building. But if it embeds you into local flow, it multiplies your power.

Appraisal for legacy also requires future-proofing. What happens if zoning laws change? If property taxes rise? If development increases pressure to sell? Families must evaluate legal protections, homestead exemptions, trust structures, co-ownership models, land use regulations, that safeguard continuity. A home worth buying is one that can be kept, defended, and enriched across decades, not one vulnerable to financial or legal erosion.

Spiritual alignment is the final, often unspoken, layer of legacy appraisal. Does the home offer peace? Does it nourish your values, not just through architecture, but through energy? When you walk in, does it feel like a space where healing can happen? Can celebration occur without interruption? Can grieving be held without shame? These questions are hard to quantify, but impossible to ignore. A home's value lives in its capacity to carry soul.

In the end, a legacy-worthy appraisal model honors everything that market comps ignore. It sees through inflation. It respects culture. It protects family rhythm and community truth. It prioritizes ownership that extends beyond one generation. And when buyers build from this foundation, they don't just acquire property, they take root.

Part Four

Collective Value—Community-Driven Appraisal And The Power Of Local Definition

In neighborhoods long subject to neglect, displacement, and erasure, the question of property value has always felt like a weapon, wielded not by the people who live there, but by external systems built to quantify what they never cared to understand. Appraisers sweep through with clipboards, comparing square footage, sale prices, and aesthetics without acknowledging the heart of the block. Bankers approve or deny loans based on formulas that exclude cultural nuance, community rhythm, and generational presence. Developers assign value based on future projections, not current life. And through this machinery, residents are told where they do and don't belong.

But there's a rising truth in real estate: communities are reclaiming the right to define their own value. That truth begins with collective awareness, that the systems assigning monetary worth were never built to honor Black, brown, immigrant, working-class, or indigenous spaces. They were built to maintain control. To dictate access. To convert legacy into leverage for outsiders. When communities understand this, the recalibration begins.

A community-driven appraisal doesn't begin with comps, it begins with connection. Residents gather to ask, "What does this block mean to us?" "What stories live here?" "What do we protect when we protect these homes?" From there, they begin documenting the real worth. Not just who sold what, but who stayed. Not just price increases, but life increases. Who mentored, who healed, who preserved, who resisted.

These metrics don't show up on paper, but they live in every sidewalk, mural, garden, and tradition.

Neighborhood associations, block clubs, local historians, and cultural stewards become central actors in this appraisal model. They create archives, not of transactions, but of truth. Oral histories are recorded. Land use patterns are mapped. Buildings are celebrated not for their design alone, but for their service, churches that sheltered protesters, houses that hosted healing circles, storefronts that supported youth programs. These details reframe the lens. A property isn't valuable just because it's updated. It's valuable because it's rooted.

This framing has practical implications. Communities begin advocating for appraisal reform, not just in theory, but in documentation. They challenge undervaluations through collective counter-appraisals. They present dossiers that include cultural impact statements, community engagement scores, and historical relevance maps. They petition municipalities and lenders to honor these layers in tax assessments and mortgage qualification. They host workshops teaching residents how to decode traditional appraisal language and re-insert their own metrics.

Local business value also becomes part of the conversation. A neighborhood may have low average sale prices, but if the block includes thriving cultural commerce, reciprocal economies, and locally owned infrastructure, its value is misrepresented. Communities start including cooperative initiatives, employment patterns, food access points, and safety networks as appraisal data. They don't just rely on external validation, they produce internal truth.

Social healing is another metric. Neighborhoods recovering from trauma often show resilience through service, not always visible to appraisers focused on finishings. A home that hosts counseling sessions, hosts block cleanups, or provides safe haven for youth is serving more than shelter, it's serving restoration. When communities define value from this angle, they're stating that homes aren't just worth money, they're worth memory, mission, and movement.

Public space becomes part of property value. Parks where activism was born. Corners where music was made. Sidewalks that held generational footsteps. This reclaiming doesn't just sentimentalize, it strategizes. It asserts that appraisers must evolve, not just technically, but culturally. The community-driven model introduces equity as a core tenet, saying that fairness isn't the end goal, but the beginning threshold.

Technology supports this revolution. Residents build digital platforms cataloging local impact. They share maps, story threads, community testimonials, and visual histories that tell the truth mainstream systems ignored. These platforms are used to dispute appraisals, challenge development proposals, and educate new buyers. The block begins to speak for itself.

Young leaders carry the model forward. Students document elder stories. Artists turn value into visual declarations, murals that say, "This place matters." Organizers establish local land trusts, ensuring that value isn't just defined, but protected. And as this consciousness expands, the old appraisal formulas begin to crack. They're no longer enough. They're incomplete. They're shallow compared to the depth of local definition.

This doesn't mean rejecting all external systems. It means confronting them. Reforming them. Educating the assessors, the lenders, the investors, and yes, even the buyers. Because when neighborhoods are allowed to name themselves, to appraise themselves, to protect what they've built, the game shifts. The price no longer tells the full story. The story tells the price.

Appraisal becomes activism. Documentation becomes declaration. Ownership becomes aligned, not just with capital, but with culture.

And value, finally, becomes visible.

Final Part

Living Appraisals—Designing Generational Strategy That Transcends Measurement

There is a final tier of valuation, the kind that no lender will measure, no agent will pitch, and no spreadsheet will ever hold. It's the tier of living appraisal. The kind that doesn't stop at equity or resale but reaches into the fabric of time itself: how your ownership strategy outlives your presence, outlasts your paperwork, and leaves behind something bigger than property, a lineage. And designing for that level of truth means every choice must be grounded in generational thinking.

A living appraisal is built around continuity. Not whether the house will rise in market value next year, but whether it will serve as a stable launchpad for two, three, even four generations forward. It includes financial planning, architectural decisions, cultural alignment, and community legacy. You stop seeing the house as a transaction and start seeing it as a trust. Not the legal kind, but the soul kind.

You begin with transferability. Can this home pass down seamlessly, not just on paper but in lived rhythm? That means creating clear titles, establishing wills or trusts, and teaching family members what stewardship looks like. It's not enough to say, "I'll leave this to my kids." You must ensure they understand why the property matters, how it's protected, and what traditions live inside it. You're building a memory machine, one that holds story as tightly as it holds structural integrity.

Financial sustainability must follow. A home that burdens the next generation is not a legacy, it's a liability. That means appraising the house for its cost of carrying, not just its sticker price. Are taxes stable? Is insurance affordable? Are utilities aligned with seasonal income cycles? Are repair costs foreseeable and budgeted? The value of a home increases when future owners won't need to scramble or sacrifice to retain it.

Then there's spatial evolution. Living appraisals include the adaptability of the home to shifting generational needs. Can the home accommodate new children? Can rooms be converted without destroying functional flow? Can aging in place be supported without displacing family rhythm? These aren't side notes, they're core to the strategy. Because homes must evolve to match the bodies, the dreams, and the complications of those who inhabit them.

Cultural and spiritual resilience form the next layer. Does the home provide freedom of expression for each generation's way of being? Does it allow the altar to shift, the rituals to deepen, the gatherings to stretch without shame or restriction? Can the next generation redecorate, reimagine, and reclaim the space while honoring its roots? A valuable home is one that remembers without controlling. That kind of elasticity, allowing change without erasure, is critical to long-term function.

Community retention becomes a strategic priority. Can the family remain engaged with the block, the local systems, the surrounding institutions for decades to come? Are there protections against displacement, rising taxes, speculative pressures, or cultural dislocation? Smart buyers begin building local alliances the moment the contract is signed, connecting with block associations, attending city meetings, supporting neighborhood coalitions. Because your home is never an island. It must be woven into the tapestry that sustains your family and protects your neighbors.

Educational continuity also counts. Does the home offer proximity to institutions that evolve with children, not just physically, but emotionally and intellectually? Does it provide safe passage to school, access to mentorship, and routes to future opportunity? Legacy-minded buyers consider not just the quality of current schools but the historical trajectory: whether the district has shown signs of reform, investment, and community partnership. If not, they advocate early, because a home that isolates learning compromises its long-term worth.

Health access must be accounted for. Is there proximity to hospitals, clinics, mental health services, and wellness infrastructure that serve all ages? Can elders access care without being uprooted? Can children receive preventive services near their home? A living appraisal includes this map, not just distance, but dignity. You assess how care is delivered locally and whether it aligns with your family's needs and values.

Preservation of language, food, celebration, and story is part of the calculus. A home steeped in cultural meaning becomes a portal, not just for comfort, but for transmission. Grandchildren learn recipes in that kitchen. Generations recite stories in that living room. Holidays ground themselves in those walls. If the architecture allows these traditions to breathe, the home becomes more than shelter, it becomes sanctuary. Buyers must design for this, not hope it emerges.

Environmental strength joins the model. Climate resilience, resource conservation, and land stability factor into generational success. Are materials durable? Is the foundation secure? Is the home energy efficient across income cycles? Is landscaping sustainable and protective? Does the home respect the natural rhythms of its surroundings, sunlight, wind, water flow, heat regulation? If so, its value will rise not just financially, but functionally.

Digital preparedness matters in modern legacy. Is the home equipped for remote work, learning, communication, and community engagement? Can it support the evolving technological needs of each generation, from aging elders needing telemedicine, to young adults launching online businesses or creative networks? Buyers now build legacy by embedding connectivity in physical space, not as luxury, but necessity.

Finally, living appraisal includes emotional lineage. Does the home remember you after you leave? Does your spirit echo through its corners? Will your children walk through the doorway and hear the past guiding the future? Will visitors sense alignment between architecture and ancestry? You're designing more than durability, you're crafting emotional permanence.

That kind of value can't be printed, pitched, or profited off. It's lived. Protected. Sharpened through every decision you make, from what you repair, to how you gather, to when you teach. A home doesn't just house you, it holds you. And if it holds you fully, then its value is already infinite.

CHAPTER SEVEN

NEGOTIATION IS SURVIVAL

Part One

Tactics For Negotiating Properties In Struggling Areas

In struggling neighborhoods, real estate becomes a different language. Sellers speak from history, buyers move from urgency, and agents juggle optimism with market fragility. The numbers don't tell the full truth, and the listing rarely reflects the lived reality. In these spaces, negotiation isn't a bonus skill, it's survival. It's how you protect your future, honor your principles, and secure property without becoming another casualty in the system's performance.

Negotiating in distressed areas means you must abandon the industry script. You're not negotiating with spreadsheets, you're negotiating with people often balancing grief, pressure, exhaustion, and uncertainty. A seller may be offloading a family property they inherited under traumatic conditions. An agent may be attempting to close deals in a zip code that lenders avoid. And the home itself may be caught between cosmetic renovation and decades of neglect. So what do you do? You slow down, strip the presentation to its roots, and shape the deal on your terms.

Start with empathetic precision. That means approaching the conversation with both data and dignity. You present the comps—yes—but not as confrontation. You say, "Based on recent sale patterns and the neighborhood's current infrastructure status, this asking price stands above the zone's performance." You aren't attacking, you're narrating. Sellers need to feel heard, especially if they hold emotional attachment. But they also need clarity. You become the buyer who understands both the numbers and the nuance.

In struggling neighborhoods, negotiations hinge on exposure to risk. If properties sit near abandoned lots, high-crime corridors, failing schools, or stalled development, you factor that into your offer. Not as a scare tactic, but as responsibility. "Our offer reflects investment risk due to the lack of public maintenance and active utility disruptions within a quarter-mile radius." When said calmly and with evidence, that kind of language shifts the negotiation from emotion to logic. You're showing that the context influences the contract.

You also negotiate through transactional transparency. Request full repair histories. Document every upgrade. Ask whether permits were pulled, inspectors were engaged, and whether local contractors did the work. In struggling neighborhoods, renovations can hide shortcuts. Sellers may install new flooring over rotted sublayers or paint walls masking mold. Ask directly. "Was this plumbing rerouted or patched?" "Can we review the foundation scope before final agreement?" These are questions most buyers avoid. You won't.

Contingencies become your armor. In vulnerable zones, you build offer structures that protect you from sudden revelations. Include inspection periods long enough for multiple specialist reviews. Add escape clauses if local zoning changes affect future use. Include appraisal-based adjustments in your contract so inflated seller expectations don't trap you into overpayment. Say, "This agreement holds if the appraised value aligns within 5% of listing, otherwise, renegotiation will trigger." You aren't demanding. You're safeguarding.

Learn to ask what others won't. In tougher markets, some sellers don't want certain things revealed. Be the buyer who refuses omission. Ask about liens. Ask about neighborhood associations. Ask whether developers are circling the block and if tenants nearby are organizing against displacement. Ask whether the seller's reason for leaving connects to ongoing political or environmental issues. Every question peels back another layer. The more you uncover, the stronger your position.

Timing is strategic leverage. In distressed areas, properties sit longer. That gives you space to negotiate creatively. Offer staggered payments. Suggest delayed closings to accommodate city hearings. Propose split escrow solutions. In some cases, you can offer partial ownership solutions that benefit both parties, especially if sellers lack the funds to complete repairs but want to retain partial interest. These structures work when framed as mutual uplift. Say, "Here's a scenario where you retain a stake while I handle the improvement and management."

Use language rooted in clarity. Too many buyers speak in generalities. You must speak like an operator. "We're positioning this property for dual use: residential conversion and short-term rental overlay, pending compliance." Or, "Given the proximity to the utility corridor and inconsistent municipal support, this offer reflects both service vulnerability and resale limitation." This makes you sound serious. Sellers recognize maturity, not just money.

Never negotiate from desperation. If the property feels wrong, you walk away. If the seller resists accountability, you step aside. If the price dishonors the context, you disengage. Because in struggling neighborhoods, ownership without principle becomes exploitation. You must choose your battles with precision. Every deal you shape defines your reputation.

And that's the final truth: Deals aren't found, they're shaped. Especially here. Especially now.

Part Two

Asking What Others Won't—Walking Away With Power

In the real estate world, negotiation is often framed as a skillset, a tactic-laden process where persuasion meets persistence. But in neighborhoods shaped by trauma, speculation, and uneven investment, negotiation becomes something else entirely: a test of moral resolve. It's not just about getting the price down, it's about refusing to enter deals that disrespect truth. And that means asking the questions no one else wants to ask.

The industry rewards conformity. Buyers who move quietly, who accept the listed price, who waive inspection contingencies are celebrated for speed and efficiency. But those approaches crumble in vulnerable areas. These neighborhoods are marked by historical disinvestment, generational grief, exploitative flips, and government neglect. A strong buyer doesn't ignore that context, they confront it. And confrontation begins with the question: What is this property hiding?

Every deal holds secrets. Sometimes it's the floodplain. Sometimes it's a history of police tension. Sometimes it's structural decay masked by surface rehab. Sometimes it's an informal tenant refusing to leave, or a past violent event never disclosed. You will not find these truths on a flyer. You won't get them from agents unless you force the issue. So ask directly:

"Has the property experienced sustained water damage at any point?"

"Were the renovations conducted with permits and up-to-code inspections?"

"Has the property ever been associated with criminal investigations, gang activity, or illegal use?"

"Are there disputes with nearby properties regarding zoning, easements, or noise violations?"

"Are any public or private entities pressuring development changes on this block that would affect ownership?"

These questions might sound intense, even uncomfortable. But discomfort is where survival begins. Buyers are trained to be polite. Agents expect passivity. Sellers lean on nostalgia. Meanwhile, the systems at play rely on silence. Your job is to break it, calmly, firmly, and without apology.

You also ask existential questions, ones that pierce beneath the cosmetic pitch:

"Why did the last family leave?"

"Has this property changed ownership more than once in the past five years?"

"Was the previous sale driven by default, distress, or displacement?"

"Do neighbors feel safe here after dark?"

"What is the city's stated development strategy for this zone, and how does this property factor in?"

These aren't questions most buyers ask. Most are too focused on finishes. On financing. On square footage. But in struggling neighborhoods, the floorplan is the last thing to worry about. What you must uncover are the fault lines, the indicators that the home, the block, or the broader ecosystem could collapse under pressure you weren't warned about.

And if your questions reveal inconsistencies, you must learn to walk away with power.

Walking away isn't retreat, it's refinement. You aren't saying "no" because you're afraid. You're saying "no" because the deal doesn't honor your standards. And when you carry clarity, your exit becomes a message: I see everything and I don't bend for illusion.

This is where emotional pressure kicks in. You may feel guilt. Agents may urge you to reconsider. Friends might say "you're overthinking it." But legacy isn't built on ease, it's built on truth. If your questions aren't answered honestly, if conditions are concealed, if your gut screams resistance, you disengage.

Understand what it means to walk. You're not walking away from opportunity, you're walking toward alignment. You're not rejecting ownership, you're rejecting compromise. A compromised purchase invites long-term regret: unlivable conditions, broken systems, unplanned repairs, community tension, safety violations. These aren't "challenges" they're structural betrayals.

Negotiation as survival also means holding silence. Ask a question and wait. Let the agent squirm. Let the seller stall. The pause reveals more than their answer. If someone is unwilling to meet your inquiry with clarity, they're telling you everything you need to know. Let silence speak. Let absence confirm what documentation attempts to obscure.

Structure your exit as a statement of principle. You don't just say, "We're no longer interested." You say, "This deal does not reflect our standards of transparency, strategic alignment, or community engagement." You remind them: You were willing to offer your money. What you expected in return was truth. If they couldn't provide it, the door closes, not with drama, but with dignity.

Then you document what happened. Every uncomfortable question, every evasive answer, every piece of evidence you reviewed. This becomes your archive, not just for memory, but for leverage. When someone challenges your exit, you show the receipts. You demonstrate that walking away was not emotion, it was execution.

The deeper reality? Walking away builds your brand. Other agents will remember. Other sellers will adjust. You'll gain a reputation for rigor. And in vulnerable markets, reputation attracts the right kind of attention, properties priced fairly, sellers committed to clarity, deals that make sense.

Because deals aren't found. They're shaped, by the questions you ask, the boundaries you hold, and the exits you execute without flinching.

Part Three

Shaping The Deal—Strategy, Structure, And Power On Paper

To negotiate is to build. And in markets often flooded with misdirection, speculation, and systemic neglect, shaping a deal isn't just about getting the terms you want, it's about engineering protection, clarity, and long-term viability. You aren't filling in blanks on a templated contract; you're designing an agreement that honors truth, reflects tension, and recalibrates power dynamics in real time. Especially in struggling neighborhoods, the paper behind a deal either protects legacy or undermines it. There's no in-between.

The first principle is customization. Standard real estate contracts are designed for ease, not accuracy. They prioritize efficiency over equity and leave little room for nuance. That's why savvy buyers rewrite them. Line by line. Clause by clause. You interrogate each section: Does this protect my position if the block shifts? Does this acknowledge environmental risks? Does this address neighborhood volatility? Does this give me recourse if city development plans create unexpected disruption?

Begin with the financial core. Traditional contracts assume bank financing, fixed closing dates, and limited flexibility. You challenge all three. In a market where property values are fragile and seller urgency may be high, you negotiate for non-traditional financing: seller-held notes, delayed down payments, staggered installments triggered by permit approvals or community stabilization benchmarks. You say, "Given recent infrastructure challenges and limited comps in the area, I'm proposing a structured installment schedule over 18 months, secured by lien and equity thresholds."

You must address appraisal ambiguity. In distressed markets, appraisals fluctuate wildly based on who's asking, how quickly, and what political or speculative pressure is in play. You build in a valuation clause that links purchase price to verified appraisal range. Not just one report, but two, ideally from separate firms with local knowledge. Say, "Purchase price shall be adjusted to remain within 5% of dual-sourced valuation assessments, accounting for environmental and municipal risk factors."

Contingencies become tactical leverage. You include clauses that give you freedom to exit or renegotiate if zoning, title, environmental, or infrastructure factors create instability. Go beyond the basics. Include language for criminal activity reclassification within 500 feet of the property, or documentation of delayed code enforcement response from city agencies. If the block has unresolved utility access disputes, that becomes an actionable exit. Contingencies no longer protect just your investment, they protect your values.

The structure must address rehab expectations. If the seller claims recent upgrades, you demand detail. Material receipts. Contractor licenses. Proof of permitting. Warranty documents. You bake in a post-closing inspection clause that allows you to activate repair funding from escrow if any component fails during the initial ownership phase. For instance, "Buyer reserves the right to release withheld escrow funds for roof replacement if leakage occurs within 120 days and post-sale inspection reveals substandard flashing or moisture barrier failure."

Include community clauses. This is unconventional, but it matters. If you're buying in a neighborhood vulnerable to displacement, you add language affirming your commitment to local hiring, preservation of architectural integrity, participation in block associations, or protections against rent hikes beyond a certain percentage. This is not performance, it's positioning. Your deal becomes a demonstration of alignment with the neighborhood's rhythm.

Clear title must be non-negotiable. In overlooked communities, title confusion is rampant. Properties passed between generations without formal recording. Liens that were never cleared. Easement disputes lost in paperwork. You demand comprehensive title reporting with legal affidavits affirming clean succession of ownership. You establish that if any defect emerges within 12 months that invalidates your rights, the seller agrees to remediation, including legal costs.

Disclosure timelines must be expanded. Standard deals give minimal time to review disclosures. You require extended review periods with penalties for omission. If the seller fails to disclose past foundational repair, flood damage, or pest infestation, they're not just risking the sale, they're risking litigation. Your paperwork needs to reflect your intolerance for manipulation. You say, "Full structural, environmental, and municipal compliance disclosures must be delivered within 7 days of contract execution. Buyer retains full right to rescind upon discovery of omitted material fact."

Use power language. Avoid passive terms like "buyer requests" or "buyer suggests." Use "buyer requires," "buyer conditions offer on," or "buyer asserts due diligence prerogative." These are not just words, they're psychological cues that shift the energy of the deal. You are no longer participating. You are shaping.

And always outline the exit. Even in an ideal deal, you must write your way out. Your contract should include clear pathways for reversal, delay, revision, and neutral arbitration. If the block suffers sudden crime escalation, if city redevelopment pushes out residents, if infrastructure collapses under negligence, you exit with dignity, without loss, without penalty. You say, "Buyer reserves the right to defer or cancel purchase contingent on public safety metrics within the designated appraisal radius, tracked through municipal reporting."

This is how you survive the deal: by designing it. Carefully. Aggressively. Transparently.

Part Four

Crafting Ownership Through Intentional Structure

In struggling markets, buyers must approach every deal like a builder, not just of equity, but of the framework that holds vision. Crafting ownership isn't passive. It requires composition. You aren't filling out paperwork, you're architecting accountability, values, and leverage into every clause. Especially in neighborhoods shaped by volatility and transition, your ownership structure must reflect endurance, stewardship, and precision.

You begin by asking: What kind of ownership serves the mission? If legacy is the goal, sole ownership may not be enough. You explore co-ownership models that include family members, trusted partners, or community allies. You define roles: who maintains, who finances, who manages repairs, who makes strategic decisions. Your paperwork defines not just possession, but participation. A property held by multiple hands needs documentation that clarifies boundaries before tension ever begins.

You also define exit strategies upfront. Not because you intend to leave, but because ownership without clarity creates paralysis. You include buyout clauses, equity sharing formulas, and decision-making pathways for unforeseen life changes, death, disability, relocation, financial crisis. You write ownership as a living system, not a fixed monument. Say, "In the event of one stakeholder's departure, equity shall be assessed at market value minus agreed-upon community preservation discount, payable in installments over 18 months." You aren't negotiating from fear, you're negotiating to keep the asset whole.

In struggling neighborhoods, ownership must reflect resilience. You design holding strategies that allow flexibility: land trust arrangements to prevent speculative displacement, joint tenancy with rights of survivorship for generational continuity, LLC structures that protect individual credit while allowing operational control. You choose not just the property, but the legal container that keeps it safe.

And you write in community ethics. Your ownership documents reflect your purpose. Whether you rent, sell, occupy, or hold, your usage must respect the block. You include clauses that restrict short-term exploitation. "No leases under six months unless approved by community advisory board." Or, "Property may not be sold above 15% of market valuation without demonstration of infrastructural investment and cultural alignment." These aren't restrictions, they're reinforcements of integrity.

You address capital pressure. If your investment requires renovation, you build in loan protections tied to progress, not promises. You negotiate draw schedules with lenders that trigger only upon code-compliant phases. You include language that allows renegotiation of terms if labor costs spike due to market instability. Your ownership agreement isn't reactive, it's adaptive. Built to flex without fracture.

Documentation includes accountability. You record every agreement, not just legal, but emotional. Families write letters of intent: declarations of why this home matters, what it protects, what it must never become. These artifacts aren't enforceable in court, but they enforce clarity in conflict. When issues arise, you return to the intent, not just the balance sheet.

Then you digitize everything. Scanned records, cloud-based backup, permission protocols. Ownership falters when documents disappear. You prevent that. You educate your successors. You hold onboarding meetings with heirs, business partners, or trusted community peers. You explain the structure in full, long before anyone needs to act on it. Negotiation doesn't end at closing, it continues as stewardship.

Insurance becomes strategic. You choose coverage that matches risk. Not just fire and theft, but floodplain displacement, wrongful eviction protection, liability coverage for shared space use, legacy clauses for asset protection. You speak with carriers about policy flexibility during social unrest or municipal failure. You document everything. If coverage gaps exist, you write financial backup plans and link them to community support systems.

Finally, you inscribe purpose. Your ownership isn't anonymous. Every deal you craft tells a story. A story of survival. Of resistance. Of intentional legacy. You place a plaque in the foyer. You host a block gathering. You include a clause inviting youth mentorship. You build a reading room. Ownership is no longer quiet, it becomes visible.

Final Part

Negotiation As Liberation—Taking Control, Building Ownership, And Redefining Power

In underserved neighborhoods, negotiation is not just about a house, it's about reclaiming the right to own without apology. It's about crafting deals that reflect history, resistance, dignity, and future readiness. Because survival in real estate isn't just a matter of dollars and signatures, it's the ability to walk into spaces others have written off and declare: This land can serve my people. This contract can reflect my principles. This ownership will carry legacy, not exploitation.

To reach that level of power, you must shift your identity. You're not a buyer. You're a liberator. You enter the process not just to acquire, but to restore. To rehabilitate truth. To protect rhythm. And that begins before the showing, before the offer, before the inspection. It begins with the clarity that you will not follow scripts designed for conformity. You will shape the process. Entirely.

Negotiation becomes self-definition. When agents say, "The seller won't accept that," you reply, "Then they're not aligned." When lenders push rigid financing, you respond, "Flexibility is mandatory in unstable blocks." When inspectors deliver vague reports, you say, "I require clarity, not courtesy." When title officers dismiss historical trauma embedded in ownership records, you insist, "Legacy must be honored, or this deal dissolves."

Every document becomes declaration. Your contract isn't just paper, it's testimony. The terms reflect your refusal to be rushed. The contingencies reflect your insistence on full truth. The language reflects your readiness to exit if even one boundary is disrespected. You include preservation clauses, community acknowledgment agreements, and post-sale accountability metrics. You reshape ownership into a model the industry has no name for, because it's built for purpose, not profit.

You negotiate with presence. You walk into meetings knowing the block's story. You reference environmental injustice, past displacement, racial redlining, and cultural fragmentation, not as complaints, but as context. You say, "This deal lives inside decades of exclusion. My offer is not a simple transaction. It's a strategy to repair." Suddenly the room shifts. You are not the buyer expected. You are building from something deeper.

You reject urgency. Real estate pushes speed "act fast," "make an offer," "don't miss out." But you slow everything down. You let silence stretch across the table. You ask questions others avoid: "What trauma lives in this property?" "What community impact will this sale create?" "What cultural displacement is at risk if I acquire?" These are not rhetorical. They're operational. And they change the outcome.

Negotiation is your refusal to dilute. You will not compromise mission to close quickly. You will not dismiss neighbors' concerns to finalize paperwork. You will not ignore zoning shifts, city council trends, or water line maps just because the bathroom has new tile. You interrogate everything. Because ownership cannot be blind, it must be built with eyes wide open.

And when you close, you do so intentionally. You host a block gathering. You speak to neighbors. You name your purpose. You post your ownership model online for others to learn from. You say, "This deal was shaped with resistance in mind. With repair in motion. With rhythm at the center." You don't just take keys, you take responsibility. Ownership becomes a living verb.

The industry may not understand you. Agents may label you difficult. Sellers may say you ask too much. Lenders may resist your structure. Inspectors may shrink from your questions. But every time you negotiate without apology, the system shifts. And every time you walk away from deals that dishonor your values, your strategy sharpens.

Eventually, others follow. They hear your story. They learn your techniques. They use your contracts. They cite your clauses. They shape their deals from the blueprint you gave them. Negotiation becomes collective liberation. Deal-making becomes cultural restoration. You didn't just survive real estate. You redesigned it.

CHAPTER EIGHT

HOW TO REHAB SMART IN HARD PLACES

Part One

The Budget Truth—Building A No-Loan Strategy That Actually Works

Rehab projects in hard-hit neighborhoods require a completely different mindset. In communities where lenders remain skeptical, equity is thin, infrastructure is inconsistent, and neighborhood stability hasn't taken root, the traditional "borrow, build, and flip" model often fails. Buyers in these zones must operate with surgical awareness, strategic discipline, and a real commitment to stretching value with precision. Especially for those committed to long-term ownership or legacy-building, a no-loan rehab strategy isn't a nice alternative, it's a survival model. And like all survival models, it demands brutal honesty from the beginning.

The first lie buyers must kill is the fantasy rehab number. Most people arrive with HGTV dreams and $30,000 budgets. They want stainless steel, custom cabinetry, walk-in showers, engineered hardwood, fresh exterior paint, and smart home technology. But unless you're sitting on deep reserves or outside funding, that list is a trap. Real rehab begins with brutal prioritization: systems first, safety next, and aesthetics last. That means the budget starts not with what looks good but with what holds the house up and keeps people alive. Structural integrity. Weather resistance. Fire protection. Water control. Electrical safety. If those categories aren't funded first, everything else you build will collapse, physically and financially.

The smartest rehabbers in struggling areas create layered budgets, not linear ones. They build what some call "phase logic," meaning every dollar spent has a sequence and an upgrade path. You might not be able to replace the entire roof this year, but patching the leak, reinforcing weak framing, and installing gutter drainage could buy you three more seasons of safety while you save for full replacement. That logic is essential in areas where cash is king and access to financing is restricted. You don't just make budget list, you make timeline matrices. You write out what you can live with now, what will cost you later, and what unlocks functionality versus flash.

Begin with systems audits. Before you buy your first screw, hire local inspectors for foundation, electrical, HVAC, water pressure, and roofing. In hard places, these systems have often suffered from either abandonment, neglect, or careless flipping. You want real assessment, not surface-level. Pay for this yourself. Don't rely on the seller's reports. You'll likely spend $1,200–$2,500 across specialists, and it will be the most important money you spend in the first phase. What they tell you becomes your roadmap. If the breaker box is outdated or overloaded, nothing else matters until that's addressed. If the water line corrodes or has root intrusion, your plans for high-end bathrooms become irrelevant.

Budget for city engagement. In overlooked neighborhoods, building departments and utility companies often operate slowly or inconsistently. You'll need permits. You'll need city inspections. You'll need engineers, maybe environmental assessments. And you'll likely face delays or unclear bureaucracy. Set aside at least 5–10% of your total rehab budget for dealing with city-related compliance. This includes fees, resubmissions, fines, and documentation services. In some markets, zoning confusion can halt projects for weeks. If you didn't budget for patience, you'll run out of resources before you build momentum.

Never begin with aesthetics, but don't ignore design altogether. Smart buyers select cosmetic upgrades that double as functional solutions. For example, instead of buying trendy vinyl flooring for visual impact, choose material rated for water resistance in high-risk zones. Instead of installing expensive lighting, focus on placement that improves security and visibility for older residents. Every aesthetic choice in your rehab should serve a non-aesthetic purpose. Paint should resist mold, not just match mood boards. Cabinetry should support family function, not just mimic catalog design. You want form to follow purpose, especially in communities where every dollar must stretch.

You must decide whether you're building for occupancy or investment. That decision impacts the entire budget logic. If you're renovating to live in the home, emotional priorities enter the equation. Comfort, identity, spiritual alignment, and generational readiness become part of your spreadsheet. If you're renovating for rental or resale, durability, neutrality, and risk mitigation take over. You select materials that resist damage, not just express creativity. You cut emotional spending and boost longevity choices. The budget becomes a reflection of your intended relationship with the property and that clarity helps you avoid costly compromises.

In distressed zones, pricing is unpredictable. Contractors may overestimate, materials may spike, and labor markets may shift monthly. That's why contingency funding matters. Smart buyers set aside 20–25% of their budget for unknowns. Not emergencies. Unknowns. A wall may hide termite damage. A pipe may rest on cracked concrete. An attic may host outdated junctions that require rewiring. These issues aren't rare, they're certain. If you didn't budget for the unknown, the known will consume your plans.

Crowdsourcing and micro-investment models can support your budget if structured responsibly. Some owners create community impact proposals, inviting friends, family, and allies to invest in the vision, not for profit, but for empowerment. They offer workshops, recognition, education, and shared legacy in return. Others pair with mission-driven nonprofits who support rehab as part of neighborhood stabilization. These models require transparency, intentional outreach, and legal clarity, but they can dramatically increase budget range without traditional loans.

Material sourcing can determine whether your budget survives. Big-box stores offer convenience but drain capital fast. Smart rehabbers explore salvaged supply centers, architectural recovery warehouses, contractor overstock outlets, and neighborhood tradesmen with surplus. You write your material list by category, and you assign multiple sourcing options per item. For example, flooring might include local mill remnants, discounted laminate, or bulk tile from nearby redevelopment projects. You don't just shop, you negotiate. You show up informed. And you never buy until you understand the material's performance history in similar properties.

Labor costs in struggling neighborhoods vary widely. Some contractors price high due to risk. Others low due to desperation. You must build vetting systems. Never choose based on charisma alone. Ask to see previous work. Request references, especially from nearby blocks. Require proof of insurance. Validate business licenses. And offer staged payment structures based on milestone completion. Labor drains budgets when buyers pay upfront for promises. Avoid that trap. Pay slowly. Document everything. Protect your timeline by protecting your pocket.

Lastly, budget for rhythm. Rehab in hard places doesn't move smoothly. There will be emotional highs, days when walls are painted, plumbing flows, and the project feels like magic. And there will be lows, days when work stalls, money thins, weather delays, and doubt creeps in. You need emotional reserves. Build buffers into your schedule. Create rituals that keep you grounded. Write affirmations in the walls before sealing them. This is more than a budget. It's a philosophy. A way of surviving repair while building legacy.

Part Two

Building Trust—Finding Local Talent That Strengthens, Not Scams

In distressed neighborhoods, the challenge of finding trustworthy labor is often underestimated. Buyers focus on budget, vision, and materials, but if the hands that swing the hammers and pull the wires aren't aligned with integrity, the entire rehab collapses. In these areas, where codes may be loosely enforced, cash often moves faster than documentation, and reputations travel by word of mouth rather than licensed portfolios, your strategy for finding talent must be built on more than hope. It must be rooted in community awareness, clear standards, and direct accountability.

Start not with ads, but with observation. Walk the block. Notice which homes are actively being worked on. Which crews show up on time. Which contractors greet neighbors, clean up after themselves, and seem to be building with intention, not just speed. Knock on doors and speak to residents who've had work done recently. Ask who they hired, how the process unfolded, and whether expectations were met. In hard places, good labor isn't found in listings, it's discovered through lived testimony. People who've survived substandard work will tell you where the trouble lies. People who've been uplifted by quality work will name names. That's your first filter.

Don't skip the vetting process. Even when someone comes recommended, verify every detail. Request portfolios, ideally of work completed within a few blocks, in homes with similar age and structural composition. Ask to see permits pulled, code inspections passed, and documentation for any specialty work, like HVAC, roofing, or electrical. In struggling neighborhoods, many contractors cut corners under the assumption that buyers won't know better. You must signal from day one that your project is not the type they can improvise. Your reputation and your safety, depend on it.

Build trust slowly and with structure. Offer clear scopes of work that define exactly what's expected, what materials will be used, what timelines matter, and how payments are distributed. Stage payments, never all upfront. For example: 20% upon materials delivery, 30% after verified completion of foundational tasks, 30% upon passing inspection, 20% after final walkthrough. This breakdown incentivizes accuracy, keeps leverage in your hands, and minimizes the risk of abandonment. Contractors may push back, especially if they're used to fast cash with little oversight. Let them. The ones worth keeping will understand your reasoning and respect your approach.

Documentation is essential. Use written contracts even for small jobs. Spell out expectations for cleanup, courtesy to neighbors, working hours, noise levels, and compliance with local ordinances. Require proof of insurance, liability and workers' compensation. If they can't provide it, you assume the legal risk for any injury or damage. Too many buyers learn this lesson only after someone gets hurt and lawyers come knocking. Protect yourself before the first tool hits the wall.

Background checks are not excessive, they're survival. Run simple verification searches on business credentials, litigation history, and unresolved complaints. Use platforms like the Better Business Bureau, local construction licensing boards, and social media groups dedicated to neighborhood rehabilitation. You'll uncover patterns, contractors who ghost clients, who sue homeowners over disputed payments, or who have a trail of half-finished projects and bad debt. Filter them out. No matter how charismatic, reputation matters more than charm.

Language matters. When interviewing potential workers, listen for how they speak about the neighborhood. Do they show respect, understanding, and commitment? Or do they mock, dismiss, and speak only about extraction? Contractors who ridicule the area they're working in will not build with care. They will build with contempt. And contempt shows up in every crooked tile, every warped beam, every shortcut taken when no one's watching. Hire those who see dignity in the block, not just opportunity.

Also pay attention to crew composition. Some contractors operate solo. Others bring teams. Ask who will actually be doing the work, whether they've worked together before, and if they're trained for their assigned tasks. It's common in distressed zones to see untrained labor passed off as skilled specialists. Don't allow it. If you hire a roofer, you want to meet the person actually applying shingles, not their cousin who's "learning on the job." If you hire an electrician, you want the licensed professional, not someone watching YouTube tutorials between outlets.

Community engagement matters too. Whenever possible, hire from the neighborhood. That doesn't mean lowering standards, it means raising connectivity. Workers who live nearby are invested in how the block evolves. Their name carries weight locally. Their work isn't isolated, it ripples. By hiring from within, you circulate capital. You strengthen relationships. You show that ownership includes employment, not just occupancy. In some cases, neighbors with construction skills may be overlooked simply because they don't advertise. Reach out. Listen. Evaluate. Build partnerships, not just contracts.

Skill development is another layer of smart rehabbing. Consider mentorship models: pairing experienced tradespeople with local youth eager to learn. Offer stipends, training access, and equipment funding. This won't replace licensed specialists for technical work, but it creates a rhythm of empowerment around your rehab. Your home becomes a catalyst for education and skill-sharing. Over time, you cultivate a crew that knows your values because they helped build them.

Transparency across the board is your shield. Post your rehab goals publicly if you're comfortable, let neighbors know what you're doing, what contractors you're using, and how they can reach you with concerns or compliments. This creates accountability. Workers tend to perform better when they know they're visible. It also deters misconduct. Neighbors won't stay silent if they see someone trespassing, dumping debris, or disrespecting the street. Use community as surveillance, not out of fear, but out of collaboration.

Finally, recognize that trust is a two-way street. Be clear. Be fair. Pay promptly when work is done right. Treat laborers with respect. Offer water, rest areas, and affirmation. If they exceed expectations, say so. Good contractors are undervalued in distressed neighborhoods because buyers often treat them as disposable. Shift that dynamic. Your praise carries as much weight as your payment.

Part Three

Design That Works—Makeovers Rooted In Function, Not Fashion

In communities where structural decay has been masked by cosmetic illusion, the only rehab that matters is the kind that restores function with precision. Buyers must abandon the popular logic of "staging for appeal" and instead commit to repairing life systems: the flow of energy, space, light, sound, and resilience. Especially in hard-hit neighborhoods, where families may face cramped quarters, aging infrastructure, or legacy trauma embedded in the architecture, your makeover must begin with the question: Will this design serve the people, not just impress them?

Rehab rooted in function starts with mapping human movement. You analyze how a family moves through space over time, mornings rushing for school, elders seeking quiet, gatherings around meals, moments of solitude, and emergencies where exit routes matter. This mapping informs layout decisions. A smart design doesn't just open rooms, it connects lives. You widen narrow passageways that feel claustrophobic. You remove awkward room splits that force people into conflict. You reorient doors to allow privacy without isolation. You build for flow, not flash.

Start with the kitchen. In struggling neighborhoods, the kitchen is rarely a showpiece it's the heart. Meals are made not for aesthetics but for sustenance and soul. That means storage must be reachable. Counters must be durable. Appliances must be efficient. You don't design around stainless steel trends, you design around nutrition and rhythm. Can a mother cook while a child does homework at the table? Can elders access items without climbing? Can the fridge open without blocking entry? These questions matter far more than backsplash color.

The bathroom becomes a health zone. In distressed homes, plumbing is often outdated, water pressure unreliable, and ventilation subpar. You focus on moisture control, accessibility, and energy conservation. You choose fixtures that can be repaired easily, not obscure designs that look good on paper but fail under real use. For families with elders, you install grab bars, non-slip flooring, and seating in showers. For children, you prioritize low-toxicity materials and temperature-regulated water flow. This is not luxury, it's protection.

Lighting must be reimagined. In hard places, natural light may be blocked by neighboring structures, aging trees, or poorly positioned windows. Smart rehab replaces dimness with brightness not just for style, but for safety and mental health. You install fixtures that illuminate key zones without glare. You choose bulbs that mimic daylight to reduce seasonal depression. You position exterior lights to deter crime and assist elders returning after dark. Light isn't aesthetic, it's psychological infrastructure.

Flooring choices reflect neighborhood realities. You reject materials that scratch, warp, or stain easily. You consider how dirt travels in homes without paved driveways, or how children's play might impact wear. You install surfaces that allow easy cleaning and reduce noise transmission between floors. If the home is elevated or sits on a weakened foundation, you select materials that distribute weight without amplifying creaks or structural strain. You don't choose what's trendy, you choose what works under stress.

Walls hold more than color. In rehab, walls are either barriers or invitations. You evaluate where walls divide people unnecessarily and where they might add needed privacy. Instead of knocking down everything for "open concept," you ask: Do the residents need separation for care? Do teenagers need private study zones? Do families need a space to gather formally, and another for rest? You design around real lives, not imagined aesthetics. And when you paint, you choose tones that regulate mood, reflect culture, and hold warmth across seasons.

Storage is rarely discussed, but always missed. In struggling homes, clutter builds from lack of storage, not lack of discipline. You incorporate built-ins where walls allow. You create under-stair compartments. You build shelving that doesn't dominate space. You prioritize safety: no sharp corners, no fragile brackets, no unreachable zones. When a rehab honors storage, the home breathes. People can focus on life, not just finding somewhere to put things.

Doors and windows serve multiple roles. In neighborhoods where safety is a concern, you install locks that feel secure but don't feel like prison bars. You choose windows with tempered glass for protection but maintain visibility. You use door designs that reinforce insulation, reducing energy bills for families who count every dollar. You don't just replace what's broken, you enhance what stabilizes.

The exterior must reflect function, not false uplift. You restore siding where needed but resist over-modernization that alienates the property from the block. You focus on gutters that control water damage. You create porches that invite neighbors, not just isolate residents. You install fencing not to shut people out, but to offer gentle boundaries, especially for households with children or pets. Landscaping favors local plants that resist drought, require minimal maintenance, and reflect neighborhood identity, not imported designs that clash with cultural memory.

Function also includes tech, but with purpose. Smart thermostats, cameras, and sensors are valuable when aligned with family needs, not just pushed for resale. You ask: Will this tech reduce utility costs? Will it help working parents monitor safety? Will it allow elders to control temperature without strain? If yes, install. If no, wait. Technology in hard places must serve survival, not status.

Functional design considers acoustic control. Can families hear each other without shouting? Can elders rest without constant noise? Can creative spaces exist without disturbing those in prayer or study? You add insulation strategically. Use rugs and soft surfaces where echo needs reduction. Design with rhythm in mind, every home has its own soundtrack. Your rehab becomes the composer.

And through it all, you build with flexibility. Hard places require homes that can adjust. You install fixtures that can be replaced without demolition. You lay tile with access panels. You wire systems with expansion in mind. You create rooms that can become offices, nurseries, guest rooms, or therapy zones. Because you don't just rehab for today, you design for what may come: change, growth, crisis, and celebration.

When a rehab holds function at its core, beauty follows. But beauty born from utility is stronger than beauty born from trend. It lasts. It empowers. It shelters with pride.

Part Four

After The Rehab—Maintaining, Repairing, And Sustaining The Legacy

Once the last nail is driven, the paint dries, and the final inspection passes, many buyers assume the rehab is complete. But in hard-hit neighborhoods, completion is an illusion. The real work begins after the tools are packed.

Because properties in these areas don't just need rehab, they need stewardship. They need a living maintenance model that anticipates wear, responds to chaos, and preserves functionality under pressure. The goal isn't just to restore structure, it's to anchor resilience.

Sustainable rehab means building systems of upkeep. Buyers must create maintenance calendars not out of luxury, but necessity. Start with a seasonal approach. In spring, inspect roofing, landscaping drainage, gutter function, and pest entry points. In summer, test cooling systems, window seals, and fire safety equipment. In fall, verify insulation integrity, storm window positioning, and internal pipe conditions. In winter, monitor heating performance, ice buildup risks, and wall condensation patterns. These checks aren't optional, they're survival mechanisms designed to prevent minor issues from becoming structural threats.

Your post-rehab model must also account for material fatigue. Even quality upgrades wear down differently in distressed blocks. Humidity can warp floors quicker. Uneven land settlement can twist door frames and windows. Old foundations may respond aggressively to newly added loads. Set timelines for monitoring: flooring movement every six months, wall seam inspection after every seasonal shift, basement and crawlspace moisture audits after heavy rains. You're maintaining rhythm, not just reacting.

Documentation is everything. Keep rehab records in a centralized format, receipts, warranties, permits, blueprints, and photographs of every phase. Tag files by system and timeline. Create folders: electrical, plumbing, HVAC, structural, exterior, interior, and community compliance. Scan and upload these to cloud storage or localized backup systems. This archive becomes your insurance, not only for legal protection, but for knowledge transfer. If future tenants or heirs need access, you're not scrambling, you're sharing legacy through clarity.

Maintenance in vulnerable zones must also include neighborhood monitoring. The health of your property often depends on the rhythm of surrounding structures. You walk the block monthly. Note changes in vacancy, demolition activity, new construction, illegal dumping, crime trends, or community organizing efforts. If a nearby house falls into disrepair, speak with owners or city officials. Partner with block leaders to report violations or offer support. Your home doesn't survive in isolation, it survives in context.

Financial sustainability is next. You create a fund, not just for emergencies, but for proactive care. This isn't a generic savings account, it's a maintenance-specific fund with monthly deposits aligned to predictable wear-and-tear cycles. If you replaced a water heater during rehab, anticipate future replacement in 10–12 years and begin saving immediately. If your HVAC was rehabbed but not replaced, anticipate failure and plan for either upgrade or diagnostic check-ins every 18–24 months. This isn't pessimism, it's precision.

You also renegotiate vendor relationships post-rehab. The contractor who rebuilt your porch may offer seasonal inspections. The plumber who rerouted your system may be willing to audit for leaks annually. Don't let those partnerships expire after the rehab ends. Build long-term service agreements, not through loyalty, but through strategy. You need people who understand your property's quirks and your community's pressures. These aren't just vendors, they're your crisis-prevention team.

Sustainability includes emergency plans. Design routes for evacuation, determine backup heating or cooling strategies, identify alternative utility access if primary systems fail. This matters deeply in hard places, where winter storms knock out heat or summer grid overloads trigger blackouts. You invest in battery backups, solar options, and community resource mapping. Know where the nearest shelter is. Know who has a generator. Know who's medically dependent on electricity so you can offer support.

For families living in the rehabbed home, sustainability must be lived. That means assigning roles for cleaning, monitoring, documenting, and reporting. Teach children how to spot leaks or cracks. Involve elders in storage rotation and safety checks. Make stewardship a household rhythm, not a silent expectation. Create maintenance rituals: monthly meetings, shared calendars, seasonal refreshes. Build muscle memory around care. A family that maintains together builds together.

Technology helps but can't replace rhythm. Use smart sensors to track moisture, fire risk, and HVAC performance. Connect your thermostat to mobile notifications. Set alerts for energy spikes. Monitor water usage to catch leaks early. But never rely on tech alone. You must walk the property. You must listen to its sounds, smell its air, feel its vibration. Buildings communicate and tech only amplifies what you're willing to sense.

Security maintenance matters too. Update locks as needed. Reinforce windows that show age or compromise. Install lighting that deters trespass but also honors neighborhood peace. Use motion sensors responsibly, not intrusively. Build relationships with neighbors who act as informal watchkeepers. Exchange contact information. Share arrival and travel schedules when trust allows. Build an ecosystem of care that extends beyond the fence line.

Community sustainability is the final layer. Your rehab is a contribution, not a disruption. That means joining local efforts for beautification, policy advocacy, service delivery, and cultural celebration. If the block is hosting a cleanup, attend. If someone installs a mural, help. If a neighbor faces code enforcement pressure, support them with resources. Your home is no longer a project, it's a pillar. Build it through visibility.

Post-rehab growth must be documented. Not just financially, but emotionally. Keep a journal of changes, how the home feels, what the space inspires, how the community shifts. Record who visited. Who blessed the home. Who challenged you to grow. This turns your rehab into a living testimony. Years from now, your records won't just show what was fixed, they'll show who was healed.

Part Five

Designing For The Long Game—Adaptability, Feedback, And Community Alignment

Successful rehab isn't just the completion of a property, it's the continuation of a relationship: between the space and the people, between the block and its history, and between the owner and their evolving role in a larger system. In hard-hit neighborhoods, where economic swings, political pressure, cultural tension, and community healing coexist in unpredictable rhythms, the smartest rehab isn't the one that changes the house, it's the one that prepares the house for change. That means adaptability must be baked into every layer of the design. And it means feedback, from residents, neighbors, and systems, must remain active long after the work is done.

Begin by accepting a truth: the home you rehab today might be lived in tomorrow by a different generation, a restructured household, or a resident whose needs differ wildly from your own. Legacy demands fluidity. If your rehab creates beauty but ignores future transitions, the property will become another relic, appealing for a moment, but misaligned with long-term use. That's why every upgrade must serve not just the resident, but the rhythm. Bedrooms should allow conversion into offices, therapy rooms, or multi-generational spaces. Closets should support storage or be outfitted for small appliances or flex use. Kitchens should include modular components that allow for expansion, reorientation, or communal preparation. You're not just building for the present, you're rehearsing for the future.

Layout decisions should anticipate aging. Even in young households, age comes quickly and hard neighborhoods age faster under stress. Incorporate wide doorways for mobility access. Use lever-style doorknobs instead of round grips. Position light switches at accessible heights. Choose hardware that allows grip support. Bathrooms benefit from pre-installed reinforcements behind drywall that allow grab bars to be added later without demolition. These details aren't dramatic, but they are the difference between a rehab that welcomes continued use and one that resists evolution.

Functional adaptability includes climate response. Hard places often sit at the intersection of environmental vulnerability: heat islands, poorly maintained drainage systems, unreliable power grids. Rehab design must include passive cooling, strategic shading, cross-ventilation planning, and insulation choices that respond to fluctuation. If AC fails during a summer spike, can the home ventilate without emergency hospitalization for elders? If insulation is thin during a cold snap, will pipes rupture or will rooms retain warmth long enough to sustain? These aren't speculative scenarios, they're regular challenges in neglected zones. Your rehab must preempt them, not just respond to them.

Feedback loops sustain growth. After rehab, create systems for ongoing listening. Survey residents on comfort, functionality, emotional wellness, and safety after six months, then yearly. Don't assume silence means satisfaction. Create anonymous drop-off points or digital forms if the home is shared or rented. If repairs happen, follow up. Ask whether the fix held, how the contractor behaved, and whether expectations were met. In hard neighborhoods, trauma often creates silence. Your job as an owner is to build trust, not just shelter.

Build block-based feedback too. Speak with nearby residents. Ask what changed when your property was rehabbed. Did safety improve? Did traffic patterns shift? Was noise contained or amplified? Did the rehab inspire others or create resentment? These questions matter. Ownership lives in relationship. You might discover your design blocked sunlight to a neighbor's garden or that your security lights improved visibility for elders walking home. These details help you refine. A rehab that isolates becomes a symbol of invasion. A rehab that listens becomes a catalyst.

Technology helps gather feedback, but only if you use it respectfully. Install systems that track usage, comfort levels, and maintenance needs, but respect privacy. If tenants are present, never surveil. Use ambient sensors, not intrusive cameras. Offer dashboards that help residents manage energy, water, and air quality, but teach them how to use it. Don't let tech become a burden. Let it become a tool for autonomy.

Expand feedback into design evolution. If a family requires workspace for small business development, explore how a storage area can become entrepreneurial launch space. If a resident begins hosting youth tutoring sessions, explore whether gathering spaces can be restructured for acoustics and visibility. Don't treat your original rehab as sacred, treat it as foundation. Be willing to change in alignment with people, not just ideas.

Community alignment must remain central. Meet with neighborhood leaders annually to review your property's impact. Share stats: rental history, repair frequency, block engagement. Ask for input: how could this house serve more? Be open to reimagining usage. A storage shed might become a pop-up food pantry. A garage might be co-opted for art or spiritual practice. Your rehab isn't private, it lives in shared space. Treat the exterior like communal canvas. Use signage, garden plots, outdoor benches, or murals that align with local memory, not just personal preference.

Legacy rehab also includes emotional adaptability. Ask whether the space still feels right. Do people breathe easily? Rest completely? Gather fully? These aren't abstract questions. Ask elders what's missing. Ask youth what feels fake. Adapt. Paint over what clashes. Rearrange what distances. Include voices in design, not just during construction, but across seasons.

Finally, record everything. Keep diaries, image collections, mapping files, testimonials. Chronicle how your rehab responds, reforms, reshapes the block. Because one day, someone will ask, What did this house hold? What did it heal? What did it teach? And your archive will answer. Your design didn't just repair walls. It preserved hope. One switch, one corner, one light fixture at a time.

Final Part

Scaling The Mission—How To Replicate With Purpose And Stay Rooted In Integrity

Smart rehab in one home can change lives. Smart rehab repeated across multiple properties can shift entire blocks. But when scaling in hard-hit neighborhoods, the danger of dilution grows. What starts as principled restoration can be lost in speed, greed, or misalignment. That's why the final lesson in rehabbing smart isn't just about execution, it's about replication with soul. It's about expanding your impact while refusing to abandon the rhythms, values, and relationships that gave your first project its power.

Scaling begins with memory. Every property you rehab must honor what worked before, materials that held, layouts that breathed, contractors who cared. You document lessons: which paint resisted mildew, which plumbing brand lasted through winter, which roof design offered cost-effective protection. Then you create a master document, not just for personal records but as a blueprint. This doesn't mean duplicating blindly. It means starting with truth and adapting from there.

You must also audit your systems. A single rehab project can be managed with spreadsheets and phone calls. But multiple properties require infrastructure: digital management platforms, budgeting dashboards, centralized communication tools for contractors and suppliers. Build a framework where every property's progress, problems, payments, and photos are captured in real time. If you're rehabbing on multiple blocks, geography becomes logistics. Without systems, stress destroys mission.

Replicate vendors only after reflection. Some contractors shine on single projects but fall under volume. Others thrive with consistency and clarity. The ones worth scaling with are those who understand your values, not just your schedule. Hire slow. Train intentionally. Write contracts for ongoing collaboration, not one-offs. Consider exclusive agreements with incentives, contractors who meet budget, pass inspection, and receive community praise gain access to additional work and bonuses. You aren't just paying for labor, you're investing in character.

Location strategy must include cultural mapping. Don't rehab randomly. Study which blocks have anchor institutions, churches, schools, barbershops, gardens and choose proximity intentionally. When your properties surround cultural infrastructure, your impact multiplies.

Tenants or residents feel connected. Crime decreases. Trust builds. Your rehab becomes part of a web, not a solitary event.

Every property in your portfolio must be differentiated without being divisive. You may shift design language slightly based on structural need, but don't create visual hierarchy. Rehabbed homes shouldn't say, "These residents deserve luxury, those deserve basic shelter." They must all whisper care. Even when budgets vary, finishes reflect dignity. Uniformity isn't required, respect is. That respect is architectural, psychological, and visual.

Create a rhythm of storytelling across properties. Document each rehab not just with invoices and permits, but with narrative. Interview former and current residents. Catalog before-and-after visuals. Share the meaning behind each decision: why this light fixture was chosen, why the porch was widened, why the mural honors the block's elders. You aren't building a portfolio, you're curating history. These stories become part of public education. They inspire future buyers to build with memory, not metrics.

Community partnerships grow in importance. When scaling, you risk being seen as extractive, even if your intentions remain pure. You must inoculate against this through visibility and transparency. Meet with neighborhood associations quarterly. Share your rehabbing schedule, anticipated disruptions, and economic plans. Seek feedback on how property use affects nearby households. Include community in decisions, not just in celebration. Treat neighbors as co-owners of the experience, not by law, but by legacy.

Consider co-ownership models for certain projects. Collaborate with nonprofits, cooperatives, or community land trusts. Let them share equity, stewardship, and profits. This redistributes power. It ensures your scaling doesn't become a lone ascent, but a collective rise. Involve residents in shaping rental terms, vetting tenants, programming public space, or designing signage. Every rehab becomes a ritual of mutual uplift.

Financial strategy must evolve with scale. Batch material purchases for bulk discounts. Negotiate rate stabilization agreements with suppliers. Create a contingency superfund where each property contributes a percentage to shared risk management. If one site suffers storm damage, others help cover recovery. You no longer rehab as an individual, you operate as a network. That's economic resilience.

Maintenance and monitoring must scale too. Create roaming inspection teams who audit properties monthly. Build neighbor stewardship agreements: people who live near your properties can be trained to spot leaks, illegal dumping, electrical anomalies, and report in exchange for stipends. You design survival ecosystems, not just ownership documents.

Replicate sustainability. Use properties to build green infrastructure, solar power, rainwater harvesting, community composting. If your homes share design DNA, they can also share ecological impact. Turn unused lots into food forests. Connect gutters to underground reservoirs for garden irrigation. Create self-healing blocks, not just self-serving ones.

And throughout it all, refuse speed if it destroys soul. Scaling smart rehab in hard places means rejecting urgency when it threatens ethics. You may have funding. You may have momentum. You may have pressure from developers or city timelines. But you control the rhythm. Rehabs are not assembly-line operations. They are heart-centered construction projects with spiritual consequence. Take the time to breathe between phases. Meet with families before breaking ground. Offer blessing ceremonies. Honor ancestors who were forced out. Declare that every home you touch will be shaped by justice.

At scale, people will forget the first property. They'll forget the photos, the permits, the applause. But they won't forget how your rehabs made them feel, safe, seen, invited, empowered. That feeling becomes your brand. It becomes your shield against dilution. It becomes your blueprint for replication.

Because when you rehab smart in hard places, again and again, with care that refuses compromise and structure that refuses collapse, you're not just rebuilding homes.

You're rebuilding possibility.

CHAPTER NINE

REINVESTING IN YOURSELF FIRST

Part One

Mindset Is Your Most Valuable Asset

Before any land is bought, before any wall is rehabbed, before any contract is signed, there is you. And you are the foundation. Not your credit score. Not your cash reserves. Not your market knowledge. Your mindset. Because no matter how strategic your spreadsheet, if you enter the process doubting your right to own, questioning your ability to shape, or diminishing your value in the face of external systems, those beliefs will seep into every deal, every design, every decision. Reinvesting in yourself first isn't optional. It's structural.

Mindset isn't motivation, it's positioning. It determines how you interpret risk, receive rejection, and respond to power. Someone with a scarcity mindset sees a denied offer as personal failure. Someone with an ownership mindset sees it as redirection, recalibration, resistance to unaligned opportunity. That distinction determines whether your strategy endures or evaporates.

You must begin with narrative repair. For far too many, the story of self has been written by systems designed to erase. Redlining wasn't just about geography, it was about psychology. It taught generations that their dreams were dangerous. That stability was reserved. That ownership was not for them. Even today, ads push ideal buyers with faces and features curated to match mainstream comfort. And when you walk into a bank or a real estate office with your voice, your hair, your rhythm, your history, they may not say it, but you feel it: you're not who the system expected.

And yet, you must say, "I belong here. This land will hold my family. My strategy will hold my legacy. My voice will shape my contract."

That begins with vision. You do not enter real estate wondering if you deserve a home. You enter knowing that your ancestors built homes with bare hands, on borrowed land, in hostile climates, and still managed joy, ritual, birth, memory. You are reclaiming, not requesting.

Mindset shifts include vocabulary. Stop saying, "I hope the deal goes through." Start saying, "I'm verifying alignment before I proceed." Shift from "I'm just trying to find something affordable" to "I'm identifying assets that reflect my principles." Every word you speak out loud shapes your internal architecture. Choose language like lumber, strong enough to hold your blueprint.

Reinvesting in yourself also means clarity about your genius. No matter your formal training or lack thereof, you know something that systems can't quantify. You may know how to spot block rhythm from three minutes of observation. You may feel when the porch was built for community or performance. You may understand which homes invite intergenerational life and which ones sabotage it. That knowledge is priceless. Don't understate it. Don't discount it. When systems ask for credentials, you show lived wisdom. That's the original appraisal.

Resilience must be reframed. This chapter isn't about romanticizing struggle. It's about elevating your capacity to build inside uncertainty. You've survived enough to know that repair doesn't begin with tools, it begins with belief. When funding is thin, mindset fills the gap. When city permits stall, mindset keeps the rhythm. When blocks collapse around you, mindset looks for the window that still holds sunlight.

You also define success for yourself. No spreadsheet, lender, or market analyst gets to tell you whether your rehab "performed." Maybe the profit was small but the healing was large. Maybe the home didn't flip fast but stabilized a family that's known eviction for three generations. That's success. Stop measuring worth in speed and resale. Measure worth in impact and preservation.

Mindset shows up in negotiation. You don't flinch when your offer is challenged. You breathe. You adjust. You walk away when values aren't honored. You don't beg for discounts, you demonstrate analysis. You don't justify your presence, you assert your power. You negotiate from lived truth, not scarcity games.

Self-reinvestment includes boundaries. You say no to projects that deplete your energy, disrespect your culture, or distance you from purpose. You decline partnerships that want your labor but not your leadership. You refuse aesthetic praise if it arrives alongside economic exploitation. You're not building to be admired, you're building to be sovereign.

And in the quiet moments between deals, between paint jobs, between community meetings, you return inward. You ask: Does my strategy still reflect who I am becoming? Does my home honor who I've always been? Does this block feel like a bridge or a battleground? Those questions recalibrate your compass.

Because mindset, at its highest form, becomes movement. It informs your walk. Your voice. Your pacing. Your ability to speak justice into architecture. And when others look to you and say, "How did you build that legacy?" you won't point to bank statements or blueprints. You'll say, "I started with belief. I shaped with clarity. I protected with rhythm. I owned, with mindset first."

Part Two

Self-Worth, Legacy, And Ownership As Healing Practice

There is a truth rarely spoken in real estate: every transaction, every tool, every blueprint, rests on a foundation of emotional weight. Because ownership, particularly in communities shaped by displacement, historical trauma, and systemic exclusion, carries a burden that numbers cannot measure. The process of buying, building, rehabbing, and claiming space is not just strategic, it's deeply personal. And for many, it is healing. Not cosmetic. Not performative. But cellular, spiritual, ancestral healing. That kind of restoration requires self-worth at the center. Because if you don't believe you deserve to own, no rehab will feel whole. No contract will feel binding. No property will feel like peace.

To reinvest in yourself is to confront the voice that says, this might not be for me. The voice formed from years of denied credit, evicted relatives, abandoned schools, unsafe sidewalks. The voice reinforced by television that never shows your family owning land, your dialect leading deals, your design language defining the market. It's the voice that whispers compromise instead of clarity. And the only way to silence it is through ritual.

You create a self-worth ritual to start each season of ownership. Before the paperwork is signed, you sit with your intention. You ask: What do I want this space to hold? What will it protect? Who will it heal? What lie about myself must be undone by this journey? You write those answers down. You read them during construction. You revisit them during setbacks. These words become your internal contract, one deeper than any legal document.

Legacy is born from alignment. Not inheritance. Not profitability. Alignment. Your property reflects not just what you have, but what you value. That means every decision, materials chosen, contractors hired, layout designed, neighborhood selected, must pass through your internal lens. Will this choice make me feel more rooted? More expressed? More generationally connected? If the answer is no, pause. No matter how efficient. No matter how attractive. Self-reinvestment is slow, deliberate, sacred.

Ownership becomes a form of storytelling. You choose not just what to own, but what story that ownership will tell. Some properties are chosen to rewrite family patterns, moving from rental instability to long-term rootedness. Others are selected to host community gatherings, cultural preservation, healing retreats. Still others stand as a line of resistance against gentrification or cultural erasure. The story is yours to write. But it must be written on purpose.

To own is to reclaim time. Systems have stolen hours, days, years, forcing families to move, rebuild, restart. Every time you choose to own with self-worth, you take back time. You allow children to grow in one room. Elders to remember in one kitchen. You create spatial continuity, which leads to emotional safety. That safety is healing. You can hear yourself in silence. You can rest without surveillance. You can cry without hiding. That is self-reinvestment in its most complete form.

Healing through ownership also requires forgiveness. You may have made past decisions that hurt your journey: overspending, partnering with the wrong people, accepting deals that felt wrong, avoiding responsibility. Let it go. Learn and release. Ownership isn't a performance of perfection. It's a process of evolution. Every mistake becomes material. Every regret becomes refinement.

You also forgive systems, but without forgetting. You see what banks did to your community. What developers did to your elders. What city zoning did to your childhood. And you choose to reclaim without being consumed. You say, "I see you. I survived you. I own anyway."

Self-worth transforms contracts. You stop reading them from a place of fear. You read them with scrutiny, expectation, and power. You edit. You demand clarity. You refuse rushed closings. You ask for proof. You don't say yes until your body agrees. And when your voice trembles, you pause. Ownership is not about speed. It's about sovereignty.

Legacy work includes ritual design. When the property is acquired, you don't just decorate, you anoint. You gather people who see you fully. You speak your vision aloud. You bless the walls. You name the rooms. You take a photo with your family holding the keys, and you write what you reclaimed. That image isn't just for memory, it's for momentum. When doubt returns, you'll look at it and say, "We did that. We deserve that. We'll keep building."

Healing must be ongoing. You take time each season to reflect: Is this home serving my growth? Am I honoring the dream? Am I hiding from myself in this space, or allowing truth to live here? You make shifts as needed. Rearrange rooms. Change colors. Host new rituals. Spaces must evolve with your spirit. The walls aren't just wood, they're witnesses.

Part Three

Systems Don't Define Your Worth—Your Ownership Refuses The Script

Systems have spent generations drawing lines around worth. They assign numbers to identity, credit scores, school ratings, income brackets, census codes and then package access accordingly. They say where you can live, who you can partner with, what you can afford, and how you should behave once you get inside. But if you accept those metrics as truth, you begin to shape your dreams inside someone else's boundary. Reinvesting in yourself first means dismantling that frame. It means deciding that ownership is not just for those who fit a formula, but for those who choose to move with clarity, even when the system doesn't expect it.

Real estate systems are built on selective gatekeeping. Lenders ask for financial histories shaped by environments they never bothered to fund. Brokers gravitate toward buyers with culturally familiar rhythms and language. Appraisal models punish neighborhoods for evolving in ways that don't resemble the suburbs used to train their algorithms. And city planning decisions favor what looks controlled, quiet, predictable, not what reflects real life.

Yet here you are. Not conforming. Not waiting. Not asking. Building anyway.

To own with integrity, you must unlearn the performance. You're not showing up to be approved, you're showing up to assess whether this opportunity honors your values. You flip the dynamic. You say, "My strategy is grounded in impact. My documentation reflects clarity. My offer isn't a request, it's a statement." When banks hesitate, you restructure. When agents resist your directness, you reframe your intent. When the block seems unsure how to respond to your rhythm, you ground yourself until alignment arrives.

Systemic conditioning will try to make you small. You may hear phrases like, "Be realistic," "Just get your foot in the door," or "Don't be too picky in this market." But when you accept low standards, you perpetuate low expectations. Instead, you affirm that your time, labor, and presence are worthy of respect. You design terms that protect your process. You question pressure. You walk from deals built on panic. Your ability to pause is proof of self-worth. Not everyone will understand. That's fine. Your ownership doesn't need applause, it needs authenticity.

The home you acquire must carry your refusal. It must reflect your pivot from approval to purpose. That shows up in every detail. You choose finishes that serve your culture, not just resale potential. You select contractors who honor your story, not just timelines. You name your rooms after your mission, not someone else's layout. Maybe the dining area becomes a space for community ritual. Maybe the hallway hosts photographs of generational healing. You design knowing this: your presence isn't a transaction, it's transformation.

You also challenge the hierarchy of scale. Systems push the idea that big is better. But one well-stewarded property may do more for your legacy than ten rushed acquisitions shaped by exhaustion. Your pace reflects your worth. You take time to verify zoning. You sit with neighbors before you begin demolition. You map block history before choosing your paint. You aren't moving slow, you're moving right.

Every decision becomes self-reclamation. You budget with transparency. You vet vendors with rigor. You honor your emotional signals when something feels off. And when a contract arrives with language meant to obscure, you send it back annotated, edited, reframed, ready for dialogue. You don't need fluency in legal codes to speak clarity. You ask questions until the paperwork reflects alignment. And if it doesn't, you pause. Because what you build must reflect who you are becoming.

That becomes your reputation. In systems used to compliance, your discernment stands out. Word travels: this buyer moves differently. This owner doesn't compromise. This rehabber listens. This landlord protects. And over time, your process becomes a model, one others watch, follow, refine. You didn't need their validation. But your refusal became their roadmap.

Part Four

Ownership As Identity—Moving Through Property With Presence

Ownership isn't just about location, aesthetics, or leverage. It's about embodiment. When you walk into your home, whether rehabbed or rented, inherited or newly built, you're not just stepping into square footage, you're stepping into a reflection. Of who you are. Of what you protect. Of how your choices express a truth the system refused to name. Ownership becomes a container for your identity, not your performance. And every room must whisper it back to you.

Too often, people acquire property by mimicking the presentation styles they see in catalogs or listings. Stainless steel everything, all-white interiors, minimalist designs that erase cultural footprint. But this erasure is not neutral, it's political. It tells residents, "To be taken seriously, you must decorate like everyone else." You reject that. You choose design elements that honor memory, signal pride, welcome ritual, and represent a palette rooted in rhythm, not compliance.

Identity flows through how you use space. Maybe you turn the dining room into a storytelling circle. Maybe you reshape the living room to hold intergenerational strategy meetings for your community. Maybe your walls become archives of family struggle and triumph. Maybe your front porch isn't just for sitting, it's for watching the block breathe. Ownership, when aligned with self-worth, treats every wall like language. Every floor like expression. Every window like worldview.

Your rituals expand. You light candles before negotiation calls. You play certain music when writing real estate contracts. You walk each room with intention before hosting community. Ownership stops being passive, it becomes presence. You don't just decorate, you anchor. You don't just paint, you affirm. You choose scents, colors, patterns that communicate emotional needs and cultural truths. That choice is healing. Because for too long, people were forced to occupy spaces designed to mute them.

Even your tools reflect identity. You don't hire blindly, you choose collaborators who speak your language of purpose. You don't rehab with generic aesthetics, you design environments that uplift your story. You don't let function override heritage, you allow both to live together. That balance teaches future generations that ownership is not just shelter, it's selfhood.

You also defend your space with spirit. If policies threaten the block, you gather neighbors in your backyard. If misinformation circulates, you open your doors to host truth-telling sessions. If youth need sanctuary, your home becomes a place of safety. You don't need to be an activist to resist. Ownership itself is resistance when practiced with intention.

And through that resistance, your identity deepens. You name your style. You evolve your strategy. You learn to say, "This corner of the home will hold reflection. This hallway will carry laughter. This kitchen will feed justice." You develop spatial language that transforms architecture into empowerment.

Part Five

Owning With Influence—Modeling Power And Possibility For Others

When you reinvest in yourself, the impact doesn't stay inside your walls. It spreads. Ownership becomes more than personal, it becomes a mirror and a model. People watch you. Not always with words. Sometimes with quiet observation. They see the way you step into meetings, the way you respond to disrespect, the way you light your home with pride, not performance. And whether they say it out loud or not, your process gives them permission. Permission to question. To challenge. To build. To dream. To lead.

Your ownership becomes influence not because it's flashy, but because it's authentic. You're not pretending to have every answer. You're showing that having clarity is enough to begin. You share your struggles, delays, denials, doubts. You speak transparently about the moments that almost broke your momentum. And in doing so, you build trust. You show that real power doesn't come from hiding flaws, it comes from refining through them.

You begin to shift what people expect from property ownership. In neighborhoods where rehab is associated with gentrification and displacement, your presence feels different. You center elders. You uplift local talent. You host block cookouts that invite, not exclude. You invite artists to paint your fence with messages of healing. You show youth how to wire a room or seal a window. You say, "This isn't just mine. This is ours." And by reshaping ownership as communal rhythm, you dismantle centuries of isolation.

Influence also shows up in your frameworks. You teach people how to read contracts, not just sign them. You walk someone through their first property tax appeal. You share how you negotiated for a post-sale repair clause. You text someone a contractor's contact info after they vent about being scammed. These actions may seem small. But they create ecosystems. Because every owner who moves with knowledge becomes a node of empowerment.

You share your mistakes too. You talk about the vendor who ghosted mid-job. The appraisal that came back skewed. The funding deal that collapsed at closing. And you narrate how you responded. You show others that survival isn't just getting it right, it's refusing to be defined by what went wrong. That mindset becomes contagious. Your circle grows. Strangers DM you for guidance. Block leaders invite you to planning meetings. Your name becomes synonymous with possibility.

Modeling influence also means holding boundaries. You don't stretch yourself thin trying to fix everyone's property. You teach them how to fix their own. You refuse to be used. You collaborate, not co-sign chaos. You protect your time. You say, "I'll help you map this strategy, but you have to do the walk." That kind of leadership respects autonomy. It affirms agency. It makes support sustainable.

You develop resources. Maybe you publish your blueprint. Maybe you host a workshop in the rehabbed garage. Maybe you partner with a local school to teach youth about real estate through storytelling and site visits. Maybe you record voice memos that help people center themselves before tough negotiations. Your methods expand, but they stay aligned. You don't dilute for reach. You refine for relevance.

And quietly, your ownership shifts the psychological landscape. People stop saying, "I could never own." They say, "Let me try a different way." They stop asking, "Do I qualify?" They start asking, "What systems do I need to challenge?" That shift matters more than any mortgage approval. Because when mindset moves, legacy follows.

Part Six

Creating Emotional Wealth—Sustaining Your Value Across Seasons

Property changes. Markets shift. Block dynamics evolve. But the most powerful asset you hold is your emotional wealth: the collection of wisdom, clarity, and identity that continues to grow no matter what building you occupy or what paper you sign. Reinvesting in yourself isn't just a strategy for acquisition, it's the structure that sustains your vision through triumph, tension, and transition. Emotional wealth turns ownership into continuity.

Begin with self-honoring rituals. You don't wait for milestones to celebrate yourself. You create rhythms, monthly, seasonal, annual—that recognize your endurance, your growth, your strategy. Maybe you light a candle for each property rehabbed. Maybe you journal lessons from every negotiation. Maybe you sit in your favorite room and speak a blessing into its corners. These aren't just feel-good moments, they're anchors. They remind you that ownership isn't just an economic exercise. It's sacred architecture.

You cultivate spaces for reflection. A home becomes an emotional archive when you treat it like a storyteller. Your walls hold decisions. Your floors remember footsteps. Your ceilings carry intentions. You set aside time to listen. Maybe you walk through each room after a difficult moment and ask yourself what's shifting. Maybe you redesign areas not just for functionality, but for healing. A hallway becomes a peace corridor. A closet becomes a grief sanctuary. You give yourself permission to adapt, not out of trend, but out of truth.

Emotional wealth includes grace with uncertainty. There will be losses, missed deals, unexpected bills, neighbors who disappear, structural issues you didn't see coming. Instead of collapsing inward, you treat uncertainty as part of your curriculum. You ask, What does this reveal about my boundaries? My resilience? My team? My preparation? You meet stress with reflection, not reactivity. And with every challenge met in truth, your emotional wealth grows.

Legacy thinking includes emotional sustainability. Who will carry the vision if you step away? Have you documented not just your systems, but your story? Have you written your ownership philosophy for future leaders? You can record voice memos. Draft letters. Leave a legacy book in your home that explains not just what you built, but why. That book becomes currency for the next generation, not just instructions, but intention.

Self-reinvestment demands pause. You create rest, not as reward, but as ritual. You don't wait until burnout forces you to stop. You build rest into your ownership flow. Morning tea alone. Silent drives through neighborhoods. Art nights with friends in rehabbed spaces. The strength of your ownership is reflected in how gently you treat the hands that hold it.

Emotional wealth is also about compassion for your process. Maybe you took longer than you thought. Maybe you overspent. Maybe you doubted yourself and missed an opportunity. So what? You return to the mirror. You name the lesson. You deepen your rhythm. Ownership is not a competition. It's choreography. Every step teaches something, even the ones that felt misaligned.

And in time, emotional wealth becomes legacy currency. When your children inherit property, they also inherit emotional clarity. When your partners review your systems, they also feel your rhythm. When your community enters your space, they don't just see design, they feel dignity. That's what ownership makes possible when built from self-worth: it turns concrete into compassion. And it keeps building, even when you're resting.

Final Part

Becoming The Asset—Your Self Is The First Property You Protect

Ownership doesn't begin with land. It begins with you. The decisions you make. The values you hold. The presence you carry. Property might be physical, but worth is personal. Reinvesting in yourself first means understanding that before any title passes, any rehab begins, any legacy unfolds, you are the original structure. The asset that cannot be foreclosed. The blueprint that cannot be stolen. The foundation that makes all other ownership possible.

Becoming the asset requires discipline. You track your energy like you track expenses. You assess emotional returns like you would equity growth. You maintain your boundaries like you maintain your roof. You evolve, not randomly, but in phases, just like a rehab. You take inventory each season: where am I leaking? What systems need reinforcement? What rituals need expansion? This isn't metaphor. It's infrastructure. Because a neglected self leads to a collapsed mission.

You assert your value across spaces. In meetings. On calls. During walk-throughs. In conversations with lenders, agents, partners. Your worth is not conditional on their tone. You don't shrink when misunderstood. You recalibrate. You reframe. You repeat your terms until they land. You don't chase inclusion, you build invitation. And when someone says you're difficult, you reply, "I'm precise." Because precision is protection. And protection is power.

You archive your growth. Not just wins. Evolution. The way you handled a rejected offer without spiraling. The time you walked away from a tempting deal that violated your values. The way you edited your own strategy after realizing a past decision was shaped by fear. These moments aren't just memories, they're proof of emotional liquidity. Your adaptability, reflection, and alignment carry currency systems can't see. But they build the wealth that lasts.

You teach through presence. When others ask how you built your portfolio, you start with mindset. When people ask how you stayed anchored during chaos, you reference your rituals. When mentees ask what matters most in real estate, you point inward, not at spreadsheets, but at self-worth. You teach that the most important closing isn't the contract, it's the closing of the gap between who you were and who you're becoming.

You leave behind more than property. You leave behind frameworks. Writing. Models. Debriefs. Stories. Strategies. You curate a body of wisdom that others can inherit without ever occupying your exact footprint. Your life becomes a toolbox. Not curated for applause, but designed for utility. Someone will use your blueprint to raise a child with stability. Someone will use your negotiation script to prevent exploitation. Someone will use your walk-away story to protect their dream.

You own with grace. Not because you've never made mistakes. But because you own them too. You integrate past versions of yourself into your rhythm. The builder. The healer. The doubter. The visionary. You host every self in your own legacy. They sit around your table. They don't compete, they collaborate. This is your home, now. And it's built well.

CHAPTER TEN

OWN THE NARRATIVE, OWN THE KEYS

Part One

Turn Your Real Estate Story Into A Movement

Real estate isn't just about buildings. It's about narratives. And the moment your story touches more than your personal goals, when it echoes across blocks, generations, and systems, it becomes a movement. Branding isn't logos or slogans. It's the embodiment of belief. When you own with intention, rehab with rhythm, negotiate with clarity, and teach with transparency, you are more than a participant. You are a cultural architect. And your brand must reflect that power.

Branding your belief begins with declaration. You write the headline of your mission, not just for others, but for yourself. Is your work about cultural preservation? About legacy for families locked out of equity? About teaching others how to invest without exploitation? About defending neighborhoods from development erasure? You name it. That declaration becomes your compass. Every post, property, partnership, and promotion must pass through its filter: Does this reinforce my belief or dilute it?

You identify your origin moment. Not the day you signed your first deal. The day you realized real estate could be resistance. Maybe it was watching your grandmother lose her home to a system that never valued her labor. Maybe it was surviving a predatory lease. Maybe it was helping a friend avoid eviction. That moment lives at the core of your movement. You shape it into story. You speak it aloud. You write it clearly. When your audience hears that story, they won't just see a business. They'll see themselves.

Branding expands through consistency. Your website, your speaking engagements, your visuals, your language, everything echoes the belief. If you rehab homes for generational families, your colors reflect warmth, continuity, and strength. If you challenge market exploitation, your tone reflects rigor, resistance, and clarity. If you host workshops for youth, your symbols reflect possibility, education, and rhythm. You don't mimic popular branding. You build your own semiotic system, your own language of impact.

Part Two

Documenting And Sharing Your Mission—Building Presence With Precision

To turn belief into movement, your story must live where people can feel it, not just hear it. That requires documentation: bold, clear, intentional storytelling that breaks past silence and reshapes perception. It's not enough to build a property with purpose. You must share the philosophy behind it. Broadcast the methodology. Archive the transformation. Because documentation, when done correctly, doesn't just inform, it inspires. And in real estate, especially when operating in neighborhoods historically silenced, your content becomes testimony.

Start by defining your mission artifacts. These are the core items through which your belief flows: your ownership story, your community ethos, your design language, and your impact framework. Each of these deserves articulation. You write a manifesto that outlines why you rehab the way you do, where your strategy came from, what your properties protect, and what false narratives you're correcting. This isn't copywriting. It's cultural clarity. Treat it like sacred scripture, your movement's origin text.

Create your movement map. This is a visual overview of every property touched, community engaged, workshop hosted, policy challenged, and legacy built. The map isn't static. It grows. Pin drop each location, overlay the impact, link the narrative. If a block was preserved from speculation because of your education work, note it. If a family stayed rooted because you refused to sell at inflated rates, archive that. This map becomes your movement's geography, where your philosophy reshaped possibility.

The storytelling must be multidimensional. Use photography with intentional framing, not just polished angles, but process shots. Show the wall before and after it was rebuilt. Show the porch as it was rotted and then ritualized. Include community members, contractors, elders, youth. Let faces become part of your documentation. Real estate branding too often sterilizes humanity. You build the opposite. Your images say, "This land holds people."

Narrate with humility and rigor. Your captions don't perform, they inform. "This home once stood empty for seven years. We rebuilt it with local talent, using salvaged materials sourced within five miles. Now it houses a family who hosts weekly readings for youth." That's documentation with soul. Not just metrics, but mission. You layer each post with economic strategy, cultural preservation, and emotional resonance. Over time, your feed becomes an archive of principles, not just progress.

Design a publishing rhythm. Your movement must speak regularly. That means newsletters, audio reflections, visual journals, and even short-form essays. People don't just want updates, they want clarity. They want to see how your mind works. How your heart moves. How your decisions align. That rhythm becomes your branding cadence. Whether monthly or quarterly, your voice lands with weight. You're not just broadcasting, you're reinforcing belief systems.

Build partnerships with platforms that respect your message. Not every outlet deserves your story. Some tokenize. Others extract. You vet collaborators the same way you vet contractors. Will they present your work with nuance? Will they engage your audience with respect? Will they honor your voice without diluting it for clickbait? When the answer is yes, share freely. When the answer is no, build your own platform stronger.

Your documentation strategy must include long-form depth. Create a digital home, a site that holds your manifesto, your portfolio, your educational tools, your community updates. Let visitors navigate through your values. Include essays. Video walkthroughs. Real estate philosophy statements. Resource toolkits. When people arrive, they shouldn't see a brand, they should feel a belief system in motion.

Expand your storytelling medium. Record voice journals. Interview community members you've served. Host real estate debriefs. Chronicle your negotiation philosophy through podcast episodes. Speak about why you walked away from certain deals. Why you said no even when profit was high. These stories change perception. They create frameworks for those who've only seen ownership done the mainstream way.

Document conflict too. Share what didn't go as planned. The contractor who disappeared. The permit that stalled for months. The budget overrun. The emotional toll. Ownership isn't sanitized. When you narrate struggle, you humanize strategy. You model how power is built through recalibration. And in hard-hit communities, that model is critical. People don't need perfection. They need process.

Archive legacy moments. When someone cries during a rehab blessing. When a child runs through a finished room and says, "I feel free here." When a neighbor says your property made them feel safer. These aren't side notes, they're central. Document with reverence. These are the echoes your movement leaves behind. And over time, they become your brand's heartbeat.

Part Three

Empowerment Branding—Visual Truth, Authentic Promotion, And Staying Rooted

Empowerment branding is not performance marketing. It's not about polish or perfection. It's about presence. It begins with a truth deeper than slogans: your work in real estate is an extension of your values, your history, your resistance, and your hope. Every visual, every phrase, every format must echo that. Branding, in this context, is not decoration, it's demonstration. It shows who you are, what you fight for, and how you shape spaces to tell stories systems refused to honor.

Photography is an act of framing belief. You capture not just finished products but process, the elder sweeping the porch before paint hits the walls, the child tracing a floor plan in chalk, the contractor blessing the roof with silence. Visuals must reflect rhythm. You avoid sterile angles and instead focus on community presence. A shot of a block gathering speaks louder than a staged interior. A close-up of a hand painting trim with reverence says more than a wide lens on curb appeal. Branding must see people.

Color choices hold psychological resonance. You avoid trends unless they serve function. Earth tones ground the work in cultural memory. Bold palettes reflect resistance. Warm hues restore what exploitation chilled. These choices appear in logos, websites, signage, social posts, print material, not to impress but to express. Your brand palette becomes a signal: this is ownership rooted in legacy, not luxury.

Typography carries attitude. You design with weight and movement. Sharp type might convey resilience; soft curves may reflect care. A font can mirror the feel of a rehabbed home, quiet strength with firm edges. Headlines tell stories before words do. In your brand kit, every character must speak belief. You choose type not from popularity, but from alignment.

Layout decisions affect attention and mood. You structure content not as corporate hierarchy but as conversation. Flyers balance image and impact. Websites prioritize story over sales. Social posts break away from templates to invite real reflection. Your brand avoids over-designed silence. Instead, it builds visual testimony, clean enough to be legible, layered enough to be alive.

Promotion must move beyond pitch. Your calls to action don't demand, they invite. You don't say "Buy now" or "Limited availability." You say, "This space was rebuilt to restore rhythm. See how it carries legacy." You speak to values, not urgency. Your brand never manipulates, it motivates. The difference shows up in your captions, your outreach emails, your partnerships. Each sentence is a brick, building trust, building movement.

Your voice is the brand. Not a script. Not a slogan. Your actual tone, cadence, reflection, resistance. When you speak, your audience hears not just information but intention. You teach through narration. You publish stories, not ads—about how each home changed people. How each rehab transformed a street. How each block learned something through your presence. Branding becomes instruction.

You build narrative collections. Profiles of families rooted through your work. Chronicles of contractors who returned to legacy building. Journals of elders speaking blessing over concrete. These become ongoing series, shared through blog, newsletter, event panel, or mural. Your archive is living. Branding is what ties it together.

You distribute branding into the neighborhood. Not just digital. Yard signs, community flyers, booklets for block leaders. Posters in barbershops, libraries, community centers. Your visuals go where algorithms don't reach. Branding becomes physical presence. Your mission becomes print that teaches, color that affirms, language that heals.

You design feedback loops. Branding evolves when real people respond. You listen. You refine. You adjust what colors connect, what messages land, what visuals reflect truth. You don't chase clicks, you chase clarity. Empowerment branding is iterative. Each phase strengthens alignment. Each revision deepens impact.

Your brand lives in your refusal to dilute. You do not decorate injustice. You do not erase struggle. You do not sanitize your process to match industry expectations. You document the cracks, the rebuilds, the negotiations, the questions. Your brand is testimony, not template.

Your platform is not just yours. You hand it to others. You mentor youth in brand storytelling. You train emerging owners in content framing. You host design workshops for communities shaped by silence. Your belief becomes curriculum. Branding becomes a shared tool, not just a personal asset.

Your brand becomes the echo of your presence. Every flyer, every video, every sentence says: this is who I am, this is how I build, and this is what we deserve.

Part Four

Owning The Narrative—Preserving, Publishing, And Protecting Your Message

Branding a belief means securing the story. Once your message begins to move, across blocks, timelines, screens, and memories, it becomes an asset. One that must be preserved with intention, published with clarity, and protected against distortion. Especially for those building in neighborhoods shaped by silence or forced erasure, the narrative is more than promotion, it's inheritance. And branding isn't complete until that message is recorded, repeated, and safeguarded across generations.

Begin with your archive. Document everything, not just final results, but the logic behind decisions. Why you chose to install a reclaimed wood mantle instead of a commercial finish. Why you rejected investor capital for a self-funded rehab. Why your rental terms include legacy clauses that reduce displacement. These decisions reveal ideology. And your archive makes that ideology accessible. Store contracts, emails, floor plans, voice notes, photos, recordings, workshop transcripts, policy memos. Build a digital folder system: belief by theme. Ownership. Legacy. Rhythm. Resistance. Each folder becomes a chapter.

Publish with integrity. You don't need to wait for a major outlet or book deal. Start where you are. A website with essays. A podcast with interviews. A zine featuring block memories and design maps. A photo series with captions in your own dialect. If you write books, include the philosophy in the introduction. If you release educational materials, wrap each chapter with real-life examples. Your content doesn't just teach, it reclaims. Every piece must resist the default lens. You're not explaining real estate from the industry's side. You're narrating ownership from lived experience.

Create an imprint. Your publishing entity isn't just a brand, it's your cultural authority. Design a press name, logo, and style guide that carries your voice. Use it for every release. Whether it's a flyer for a youth panel or a property portfolio for legacy buyers, stamp it. When people see your imprint, they know it stands for values. Precision. Power. Respect.

Over time, that mark becomes a signal, a visual shorthand for presence that doesn't dilute.

Host exhibitions. If your work touches physical space, bring people into it. Curate events inside your properties. Showcase design decisions alongside poetry. Hang photographs of the rehab process next to essays. Invite collaborators to speak. Use these events to broadcast the brand's heart, not its market value, but its emotional worth. This strategy turns architectural progress into narrative celebration.

Protect the story. As your message grows, others may attempt to co-opt or mimic it. Some might strip the language and apply it to projects that lack depth. Others may dilute your process to fit funder agendas. You guard against this through explicit messaging. Say what you do. Say why you do it. Say what it's not. Let no partner, platform, or purchaser remix your work without respect. Empowerment branding stays rooted by staying honest. You build a terms-of-use statement for your story, not because you're rigid, but because your legacy deserves clarity.

You organize the brand into modules. Community impact. Architectural strategy. Educational outreach. Real estate philosophy. Investment ethics. Each module holds visuals, language, theory, and documentation. This structure allows you to present your movement cleanly, whether you're briefing stakeholders, training mentees, or onboarding team members. Brand modules act like building blocks. People can use them, adapt them, cite them. But they all return to your foundation.

Brand your evolution. Don't freeze your message in time. As your strategy grows, so should your visual language. You may shift color palettes to reflect new emotional tones. You may revise your typography to reflect sharper emphasis or softer edges. You may refine your slogans based on lessons learned. But every shift should reflect growth, not trend. Document the transitions. Preserve the prior versions. Let your audience witness your development. That transparency becomes part of your credibility.

Build distribution channels that bypass noise. Algorithms fluctuate. Platforms change. Engagement metrics deceive. You build your own email lists. Your own SMS strategy. Your own print network. Your own podcast channel. You partner with community radio, block associations, cultural centers. Empowerment branding doesn't wait for virality. It moves through values. That movement requires steady connection, not chasing reach, but cultivating resonance.

Continue shaping your brand through mentorship. Teach upcoming rehabbers, publishers, creatives, investors how to build not just property, but presence. Lead sessions on values-first branding. Walk them through mistakes you made. Share frameworks without ego. When you model this kind of leadership, your brand becomes school. Not just inspiration, but institution.

Part Five

Living The Brand—Walking It, Wearing It, Working It Every Day

To truly brand your belief, you must do more than publish your message, you must embody it. People don't just believe what they read. They believe what they witness. That means your brand must extend far beyond visual identity or promotional strategy. It must live inside your behavior, your habits, your rhythm. The way you walk onto a property. The way you speak at a meeting. The way you introduce yourself in spaces where ownership wasn't expected. Living the brand is full immersion.

Begin with your daily alignment rituals. Every morning, ask yourself, What does my presence communicate today? What am I affirming with my tone, my decisions, my posture? This isn't vanity, it's accountability. If your brand stands for legacy, dignity, and clarity, your decisions must reflect that. Even in small moments. Do you explain your process when mentoring a youth rehabber? Do you correct misinformation calmly in investor meetings? Do you take time to review rental terms with your tenants? Living the brand means showing your belief through action, not just announcement.

Your dress becomes part of the brand. Not in terms of trend or expense, but intention. Maybe you wear colors that echo your design palette. Maybe you choose styles that reflect cultural grounding, professional command, and emotional resonance. Even if it's a hoodie and boots, make it consistent. Make it respectful. You don't dress to impress the system. You dress to reinforce your rhythm. When people see you, they should feel alignment before they hear it.

Your voice must be trained. Not scripted, but sharpened. You practice how to explain your model in three sentences. How to respond when someone says, "Real estate isn't really political." How to affirm your legacy-building strategy when speaking to funders or community critics. Your tone blends emotional intelligence with philosophical precision. Your stories land without apology. You don't perform. You stand.

Branding belief means walking into rooms as if they were already yours, because your clarity earned that space. You enter city zoning meetings with the same rhythm as family blessing rituals. You don't compartmentalize your purpose. You bring your whole self into every encounter. That's the brand's power: it's not edited for context, it lives full-time.

You integrate the brand into your workspace. Your office reflects your values. Your walls carry past blueprints, community maps, affirmations, and letters from families you've helped. You don't decorate for aesthetics, you curate for memory. Your desk holds property records and poetry. Your calendar includes negotiation calls and healing check-ins. This isn't multitasking. It's mission coherence.

Your meetings become manifestations. Whether you're in a coffee shop with an aspiring rehabber or a conference hall with national advocates, your brand lands through how you listen, how you frame questions, how you respond under pressure. You never sacrifice values for proximity. You build respect by staying whole. If someone tries to dilute your process, you pause and return to your statement of belief. That doesn't make you rigid, it makes you reliable.

Living the brand means honoring fatigue. You pace yourself. You schedule restoration days. You protect your spiritual rhythm. Because burnout destroys clarity. You can't advocate for healing in real estate if you're constantly fragmented. Self-care becomes branding. Not in a promotional sense, but in a structural one. Your ability to breathe deeply is part of the belief you preach.

You let your team embody the brand. You train collaborators not just in technique, but in tone. You explain your visual choices. Your ethics. Your reason for walking away from easy profits. You build onboarding materials that include more than tasks, they include ideology. Every assistant, contractor, designer, strategist moves with shared rhythm. Your brand becomes a collective act.

Even your silence is branded. When you choose not to engage, when you pass on partnerships, decline offers, avoid platforms, it's because those options don't match your belief system. And you make that clear. You say, "We build legacy, not urgency." Or, "Our homes protect history, not exploit it." Your refusal becomes a statement. And over time, your boundaries teach others how to approach you.

Living the brand means building memory. You create traditions. The annual block dinner for every home you helped stabilize. The seasonal letter to your audience. The community quilt stitched from design samples and family photos. These aren't add-ons. They're rituals. They reinforce that your movement is real, not just strategic.

Everything you touch, everything you teach, everything you correct, everything you create, that's the brand. And when people speak about you years from now, they won't quote your marketing copy. They'll quote your presence. The moment they heard you say something that broke a cycle. The way your rehab made a block breathe again. The flyer that carried courage. The contract that spoke truth.

Part Six

Expanding The Echo—Your Brand As Community Framework

When you build a brand rooted in belief, that brand must echo beyond yourself. It becomes infrastructure for others, owners, artists, advocates, educators, builders, who want to walk the path but need clarity and courage. Empowerment branding isn't just influence. It's invitation. A signal that others can shape, teach, and carry presence in ways that speak their truth. You're not just broadcasting your message. You're building frameworks others can enter, reshape, and expand.

Your brand becomes a shared language. People begin to adopt your phrasing, your negotiation cues, your design metaphors. They quote your essays. They reuse your rhythm. And instead of guarding it like property, you strengthen it through visibility. You publish guides: "How to Frame a Rehab in Rhythm," "Design Ethics for Cultural Spaces," "Branding Legacy Across Blocks." These become open-source documents. You encourage remix, with attribution and alignment. Because truth doesn't weaken when shared. It multiplies.

You identify brand ambassadors. Not celebrities. Community leaders. Teenagers who organized their first block cleanup. Elders who shaped zoning protests. Rehabbers who rebuilt a pantry instead of a walk-in closet. These ambassadors become nodes in your network, people who carry and model the belief, adapted to their context. You support them with mentorship, resources, space, amplification. Your brand isn't a hierarchy. It's a constellation.

You build educational tools from your branding logic. Slide decks. Video walkthroughs. Real estate literacy packets. You show how belief shapes layout, how ethics shape contracts, how identity shapes design. These tools are distributed not just through your website, but through schools, rec centers, places of worship, trade programs. Your brand teaches quietly, consistently, and intentionally.

You co-author content with your community. Invite others to write blog posts, record reflections, curate playlists, sketch alternative layouts. Your brand becomes collaborative storytelling, not a monologue. You're still the anchor, but you're not the only voice. The diversity of contribution reinforces your original message: ownership is not static, it's collective. Belief grows stronger when others narrate it from lived experience.

Your framework anticipates transformation. You don't freeze your brand at one stage. You build versioning. Brand 1.0 served rehabs. Brand 2.0 enters development equity. Brand 3.0 expands into publishing, community land ownership, elder care infrastructure. Each phase carries prior lessons forward. You document the shift. You announce transitions. You bring your audience with you, slowly, clearly, without dilution.

You create feedback ecosystems. Not surveys. Real engagement. You host listening sessions with youth and elders. You ask questions: What parts of our brand serve you? What parts confuse or alienate? What stories are we not telling yet? What formats do you prefer? This input shapes next steps. Your brand evolves with those it claims to serve. That's alignment in motion.

You maintain a home for the message. Not just your own property, but a branded space. A gallery. A gathering house. A learning hub. A studio. A center for rhythm restoration. This space carries your logo, your visuals, your voice, but it houses others. Block meetings. Artist shows. Legacy dinners. Economic strategy circles. The space affirms: this brand is real. And it belongs to more than one person.

You protect the brand by modeling maturity. When conflicts arise, ideological disagreements, community tensions, misaligned partnerships, you respond with reflection, accountability, and ethical clarity. You don't perform perfection. You narrate growth. You say, "We missed that. Here's how we're refining." Or "Our impact didn't land as intended. Here's how we're listening." Your belief system survives because it breathes.

Your brand ultimately becomes a memory engine. Years from now, people will trace back community resilience not just through buildings or flyers, but through your frameworks. Your voice. Your visuals. Your decision maps. Your forgiveness rituals. That's the echo. That's the infrastructure.

Final Part

Legacy In Motion—How To Anchor, Amplify, And Let Your Brand Outlive You

You don't just build for yourself. You build for the echo. Because branding rooted in belief doesn't end when the paperwork's filed, the website is live, or the mural dries. It keeps moving. Through memories, neighborhoods, timelines, and tongues. Your brand becomes legacy, not because it lasted, but because it lived. In voices other than yours. In movements you didn't micromanage. In moments you couldn't predict. The final layer of branding isn't just identity. It's immortality. It's shaping infrastructure so your mission breathes long after you do.

Legacy branding begins with succession, not just in property, but in message. You design a continuity system. Not just a will, but a movement manual. A curriculum. A code. You gather the people who've watched you build, mentors, mentees, collaborators, elders and say, "This is how we did it. This is why we did it. This is what must never be compromised." You document workflows. You assign stewardship. You create role maps where others step into rhythm without scrambling. Your brand becomes blueprint.

You archive your emotional DNA. Not just testimonials, but turning points. You write about the deal that nearly broke your spirit. The workshop that turned into a healing circle. The elder who told you, "Your buildings carry prayers." You collect these fragments and organize them. A legacy book. A library of process notes. A protected drive of video reflections. These materials carry the heartbeat of your brand. They prevent dilution by preserving depth.

Amplification is organized, not improvised. You identify brand inheritors, people not just talented but aligned. You host shadowing seasons. Let them sit in on calls. Observe your rhythm. Ask hard questions. You don't train through transaction. You train through storytelling. Through correction. Through co-creation. These inheritors write their own chapters, but they cite yours in the footnotes. That's not control. That's stewardship.

You extend your brand into structural alignment. Your belief system becomes embedded in contracts, in policy suggestions, in community agreements. You may not sit on every zoning committee, but your brand speaks through language others now use. The way people describe cultural integrity. The way someone explains equitable home design. The phrasing used in legacy preservation clauses. All branded, not with a logo, but with your lens.

You model brand flexibility across decades. You teach your inheritors that branding doesn't mean freezing in time. You coach them to reframe for new audiences, new crises, new tools. But you also insist that some things do not bend. That certain values, community dignity, design for healing, refusal to exploit, must remain untouched. You create a brand code of ethics. Signed. Practiced. Protected. When people enter your framework, they know where the lines live. And why.

You anchor the brand in rituals. Annual dinners on block corners. Seasonal blessing events inside rehabbed homes. Artistic residencies in formerly abandoned structures. You create dates the community remembers. Not to celebrate you, but to renew the work. You publish "State of the Rhythm" letters. Host legacy circles. Share reports not just of profits, but of preservation. Ritual branding carries deeper truth. It reminds people that belief must be tended, not just posted.

Visual language is refreshed through remembrance. When your brand expands, you revisit your origin colors, typography, imagery. You host gatherings where community helps shape new palettes, symbols, taglines. You treat brand evolution like ceremony, not convenience. This honors what came before. And ensures that what comes next carries familiar light.

You institutionalize your brand without institutionalizing your energy. You build legacy centers, spaces for education, healing, negotiation, storytelling. You document your frameworks and publish open-access models. You may become a foundation. A trust. An institute. But never a hollow brand shell. Your movement breathes in the walls. In the signage. In the mentorship maps taped to office doors.

Protection comes through proactive embedding. You write brand protection clauses into collaboration contracts. You draft usage agreements for your content. You file trademarks where necessary, not to restrict truth, but to safeguard intention. You watch for exploitation and respond with precision. You say, "That's not alignment. That's extraction." And you enforce with dignity. Because legacy without defense becomes distortion.

And most importantly, you teach your successors not to idolize, but to innovate. You tell them, "My brand was built for a specific season. Yours must live in your own." You encourage mutation within boundaries. You coach reinterpretation within rhythm. You urge expansion with anchored ethics. You don't need replicas. You need catalysts.

One day, someone will walk past a property you rebuilt. They'll see the signage. Hear the story. Feel the texture of the belief. Maybe they won't know your name. But they'll say, “This work feels like legacy.” That’s the brand working. That’s your belief in motion. That’s your life leaving behind infrastructure, not just inspiration.

Because you didn’t just build homes. You built meaning.

You didn’t just publish strategy. You preserved soul.

You didn’t just promote presence. You made presence policy.

Your brand doesn’t end with you. It begins again with every person who says, “Because they believed, I will build.”

CHAPTER ELEVEN

CASE STUDIES & STREET WISDOM

Part One

The Buy That Rewrote The Block—A Real-World Pivot In Legacy Strategy

The year was 2017. The block was decaying. Not in the dramatic sense of crumbled roofs and headline-worthy fires, but in the quieter way neighborhoods unravel, vacant properties quietly multiplying, seniors moving out under pressure, corner stores shuttered without announcement. One home in particular had become a symbol of decline. A three-bedroom brick house with iron railings and a wraparound porch, it sat crooked on its foundation and bore the memory of something once proud. Now it whispered surrender.

On paper, the property was worthless. It had failed multiple inspections, city records marked it "non-essential," and rumors swirled that the lot would be leveled for code violations. Yet one buyer saw through the static. She didn't see erosion, she saw infrastructure. She understood that this house wasn't dying. It was waiting. For paperwork to be rewritten, for rhythm to be respected, for someone to buy not just with money, but with memory.

Her offer was unconventional. She approached the out-of-state owners with empathy and strategy. "You're holding onto a property that's bleeding," she said. "But this house still carries the story of this block. I want to restore that. Not flip it. Reclaim it. I'll offer $6,500 in cash plus documented commitment to rehab within community compliance frameworks." The owners, tired of monthly headaches and mounting fines, said yes.

Immediately, her team began mapping the story, photographs of the property as it stood, interviews with elderly neighbors who remembered the original family, handwritten notes found inside a collapsed cabinet, newspaper clippings of block parties from the 1980s. These artifacts weren't decorations, they became the blueprint. She wasn't building new. She was restoring belonging.

The rehab plan prioritized emotional function. No stainless steel. No open concept. Instead: layered paint to reflect cultural depth, reinforced porch beams to allow intergenerational gathering, reclaimed wood floors sealed with non-toxic stain, and a window installation to echo the original lattice pattern. She worked with local carpenters, most of whom hadn't touched code-permitted projects in years, and who wept when asked to reassemble the archway using their own grandparents' designs.

Financing was surgical. She didn't use traditional lenders. Instead, she created a crowd-supported legacy campaign: "Restore Memory, Not Just Housing." Contributors received community workshop invitations, monthly photo updates, and the promise of an annual block gathering. Within 60 days, she raised $32,000 from allies who understood that belief moves capital better than interest rates.

Mistakes came quickly. The city threatened demolition again after discovering outdated permits. A contractor abandoned the electrical project after payment disputes. Mold was found beneath the staircase, triggering a $4,200 remediation surge. But each setback became a signal. She restructured payment terms: 40% upfront, 30% upon milestone verification, 30% after post-community review. She rewrote her permit communication process with weekly city liaison meetings. She established a mold contingency protocol for future properties.

And slowly, the house breathed again.

Three months later, windows shone with clarity. The porch held a youth reading circle. The living room hosted community elders to discuss block revitalization ethics. The bathroom, once considered unrepairable, featured hand-painted tiles from local students telling stories about the neighborhood's roots. The house wasn't just standing. It was speaking.

The value jump was immediate. Zillow's algorithm tried to push her property to $78,000. She rejected it. "You don't appraise legacy," she said. Instead of selling, she created a stewardship agreement. A young family moved in under a cultural preservation lease: fixed rent, responsibility for upkeep, participation in block engagement, and refusal to sell without community forum. This wasn't just a deal—it was doctrine.

Lessons stacked:

Financial wisdom: Creativity trumps credit. Cash plus community allegiance created leverage the market couldn't measure.

Cultural power: Restoring design traditions reignites dignity. Every design decision echoed historic texture, not trend.

Strategic patience: Immediate problems don't negate long-term purpose. She didn't rush—she recalibrated.

Ownership as honor: Housing isn't transaction. It's trust. Her stewardship lease redefined landlord logic.

Her process birthed a brand. People began calling it "The Memory House." Real estate panels asked her to speak. Nearby homeowners asked for help copying her model. The city, once adversarial, invited her to review upcoming code change drafts for block preservation. And most importantly, the neighbors stopped whispering about decline. They started debating potential. That's street wisdom at work. That's what it means when your truth becomes someone else's breakthrough.

Part Two

Before-And-After Breakdown—How One Overlooked Duplex Became A Blueprint For Emotional Infrastructure

The property sat like a shrug. A two-unit duplex on a forgotten avenue, wedged between a chain-link fence and a concrete lot where children once played. Graffiti framed the front door. A neighbor used the back steps to stash broken equipment. The roof sagged, the windows screamed neglect, and local realtors labeled it "a liability with no upside." But what the market dismissed, a builder with rhythm recognized, this wasn't just housing. This was a stage waiting for restoration. Not cosmetic. Not commercial. Emotional.

The buyer wasn't chasing comps. He was chasing continuity. He'd grown up three blocks away, in a house that no longer existed due to eminent domain. He wanted to create space for healing. Not profit-first occupancy. The duplex represented two truths: communal grief, and architectural possibility. So when he saw the listing for $11,700, languishing after nine months with no offers, he didn't flinch. He countered at $8,000, stating he'd waive inspection but require full deed transparency and historical documentation. The seller agreed without hesitation.

Before: The interior was a catalog of abandonment. Peel-stained walls. Floorboards clawed by water damage. Kitchens gutted by scavengers. No stove. No sink. Bathrooms missing tiles and glass. A mattress lay diagonally across the hallway, soaked in mold. But amid the decay: evidence of life. A child's drawing hidden behind a panel. A grandmother's calendar from 1994. A love letter carved into wood. These became the raw material, not for design, but for direction.

Instead of starting with repairs, the buyer started with the block. He surveyed neighbors, asking: If this property healed us, what would it include? They said: a safe porch for storytelling. A shared garden. An indoor gathering space that didn't need to be rented. A reading nook for children. The rehab plan took shape, not from blueprints, but from lived need.

The front unit was redesigned as a cultural living space. Wide windows returned, but with reinforced framing. Flooring was reclaimed from abandoned school gyms. Walls were refinished, but painted in rich tones drawn from Afrocentric palettes, burnt orange, deep earth brown, ancestral blue. Furniture came from neighborhood donations. The living room included a soft platform for intergenerational meetings. A small gallery hung photographs of community events, block transformations, and past residents. This unit was not for rent, it was for ritual.

The rear unit became affordable transitional housing for displaced families, with a lease that integrated dignity clauses: fixed rate, no inspection shaming, maintenance-on-call with no threshold, and co-developed calendar check-ins with a social worker. The unit held quiet textures, calming lighting, sound-dampening walls, and a rotating art installation created by local youth. The bathroom included a mirror etched with affirmations, the kitchen with a chalkboard wall for family schedules, dreams, and legacy notes.

Financing was layered. No banks. No standard funding. Instead:

$15,000 from a legacy trauma grant, secured after proposing the home as a neighborhood restoration model.

$8,000 in service trade equity, local contractors worked in exchange for future property access or consulting referrals.

$3,000 in community donation, raised through block parties, story-sharing nights, and print sales of rehab photos.

A total rehab cost of $26,000 delivered two units, fully functional, deeply intentional, and built to serve rather than showcase.

After: The duplex didn't go viral, but it transformed the neighborhood's emotional terrain. People began leaving notes on the porch: "This home gave me breath." "I remembered my father walking me here." "Can my child help with the garden?" Elderly residents who hadn't spoken to each other in years began gathering for storytelling again. A mural showed up on the corner wall, uncommissioned but perfectly aligned: two hands holding bricks, with the word "Rebuild without rushing."

City officials tried to classify the home as a community facility. The buyer pushed back: "This is residential with rhythm. Let it live unfenced." Conversations about zoning reform began, not because of lobbying, but because one home refused categories.

Lessons:

Healing drives architecture. When function follows emotion, rehab supports spirit—not just shelter.

Community defines utility. The best layout comes from listening—not from software.

Money moves when story leads. Grants, trades, and gifts follow belief—not spreadsheets.

Design must echo history. Every paint choice and floor restoration carried memory—not just trend.

What was once "just another duplex" became a prototype. Nearby owners asked for guidance. Schools sent students for field studies. Researchers documented the process for housing equity journals. And every person who walked past began seeing their own property differently, not just as a financial asset, but as a space for healing, honoring, and holding rhythm.

Part Three

The Mistake That Built A Model—Lessons From A Failed Flip, Reclaimed

It was supposed to be a win. The buyer had experience, resources, a contractor network, and a roadmap. The property, a neglected four-bedroom on a historically Black block, came listed at $16,000, stripped to studs, left behind by a nonprofit that collapsed mid-project. On paper, it was the perfect canvas. Zoned for residential, approved for rehab credits, and surrounded by homeowners eager for restoration. The plan was tight: buy fast, rehab smart, rent with dignity, and use the positive cash flow to seed a youth mentorship space in the garage. But within 60 days, it was spiraling. Not from design flaws. Not from budget missteps. From something deeper: neglect of rhythm.

The buyer skipped the block walkthrough. He focused on the building's specs, square footage, ceiling height, permit history, but never sat with the neighbors. Never asked about traffic patterns, street tension, or legacy expectations. He assumed proximity was permission. That decision cost him alignment.

Mistake one came fast: the contractor team, chosen from referrals three neighborhoods over, arrived with volume mentality. They built as if preparing for resale, not occupancy. They changed the façade with vinyl siding that clashed with the block's brick heritage. They laid laminate flooring over uneven joists without consulting an inspector. They ignored soundproofing, essential for a block with high activity and elder households next door. As a result, the property felt sterile. Functioning, yes. But spiritually silent.

Like a stranger on a street that once hosted music every weekend.

Mistake two followed: promotion without grounding. The buyer announced availability on social media, with flyers that used words like "affordable" and "upgraded" but missed the cultural cues that matter. No mention of block history. No nod to community design logic. The tone felt extractive, even though the intention wasn't. Locals didn't respond. Elders whispered, "This home isn't for us." Youth laughed off the showing dates. The brand had skipped belonging.

Then came the financial pivot, an investor offered $75,000 if the buyer would sell early and exit the block. It would be a profit jump. Clean. Efficient. Tempting. But something pulled him back. A moment of silence in the living room where he stood, hearing muffled sounds of block children, recognizing that no dollar justified disconnect. He declined. Not because he was certain of the next move, but because he knew the lesson wasn't complete.

The truth landed harder the next week: a neighbor knocked, holding a photo. It showed that same home in 1983, covered with laughter. The porch had hosted a wedding. The hallway framed a local activist's first community address. "You built the walls, but not the welcome," she said. That line became gospel.

Instead of salvaging profit, the buyer committed to process repair.

He reconvened his team. Fired the lead contractor, hired a group from within three blocks, builders who knew the soil, the tension, the texture. They tore up the laminate.

Reframed the windows. Returned brick accents. Installed flooring that dampened noise for the elder next door. The porch was restructured, wider, with built-in seating, soft lighting, and planters sourced from local artists.

The garage wasn't turned into an office. It became a mentorship lab, open on Saturdays, featuring design workshops, storytelling circles, and economic literacy clinics. The branding was redone, not with slogans but with purpose: "Rebuilt with Rhythm. Occupy with Honor." Flyers included testimonials from residents. Lease terms reflected collaboration, not control.

Financial loss? Absolutely. The budget exceeded projections by nearly 30%. Timeline stretched five months past initial estimates. But what emerged was a property that lived. A space that reflected what the street taught, not what the spreadsheet dictated.

In the six months after reopening:

Block participation in cleanup initiatives rose 40%.

Youth requests for mentorship tripled.

Two nearby homeowners began their own rehab projects, borrowing floor plans and lease terms from the restored house.

The city offered zoning consultation support, unasked, unprompted.

Mistake became model.

Lessons etched in sweat and silence:

Proximity is not permission. You earn presence by listening—not showing up with blueprints.

Design without belonging is vandalism. No matter how elegant, if the block doesn't recognize itself in the property, the architecture is theft.

Brand must reflect rhythm, not trend. Your flyers, your voice, your signage, all must speak culture before commerce.

Legacy lives in refusal. Declining a profitable exit isn't weakness, it's vision. Walking away from fast money to honor slow healing rewires everything.

The buyer documented everything. Not just mistakes, but emotions. A published piece titled "The Profit I Refused: Learning From the Flip That Failed Forward" became required reading in a local real estate ethics course. A photo series traveled through barbershops, churches, and community centers. The home became a beacon. Not because it was perfect. But because it had been humbled, and risen.

Part Four

Pattern Recognition—Deal Structures, Cultural Archetypes, And Tactical Pivot Points Across The Map

Street wisdom doesn't come in theory, it lives in patterns. Case after case, block after block, the rhythm repeats: buyers and builders walk into overlooked properties, face local resistance, economic friction, and emotional complexity. Yet those who learn from the block, not just from the books, begin to recognize truth beneath the surface. What others call liabilities, the street calls archetypes. And when you see the pattern, you learn to pivot with precision.

Take the Inherited Weight Home. You'll find it in almost every city, usually a property held in emotional limbo. It once belonged to a matriarch or patriarch, now passed through multiple heirs. Often no one lives there, but no one agrees what to do with it either. The legal title might sit with a sibling in another state, while another sibling mows the lawn weekly out of loyalty. The home itself might be solid: roof intact, porch usable, no major damage. But the conversations surrounding it are fragile, loaded with family tension.

Most investors approach these homes with legal paperwork and monetary logic. The street teaches a different lesson, lead with emotional clarity and cultural respect. In one case, a buyer succeeded not because she offered the highest price, but because she brought presence. She showed up at a neighborhood church where heirs attended. She shared her own story of family fragmentation. She didn't ask for permission, she asked for trust. Weeks later, she closed below market value but gained something priceless: alignment. The family requested a mural of the original owner on the exterior wall, and she said yes. The deal wasn't just financial, it was sacred.

Then there's the Zoning-Limbo Duplex. This property straddles identity: one half of the street is zoned commercial, the other still residential. The building itself has served different purposes over time, sometimes housing, sometimes retail, sometimes something in between. Permits are tricky. Future use is unclear. Most investors avoid it. But rhythm recognizes complexity as opportunity.

One buyer refused to fight zoning. He leaned into the ambiguity. The upstairs remained residential with traditional layouts, intentional soundproofing, and community-minded rental terms. The downstairs evolved into an economic incubator, a rotating space for pop-up shops, financial literacy classes, cooperative work sessions. No zoning violations. No bureaucratic gridlock. Just design serving flexibility. Instead of forcing code change, he reframed usage through participation.

Then there's the Trauma-Locked Property. You'll know it when you feel it. The specs look clean. The pricing seems fair. But the block doesn't breathe when the house comes up. Something happened there, something the records may not show. Death. Displacement. Scandal. Violence. The air is heavy. The sidewalk hesitates. Most buyers walk away. But builders with rhythm know: you don't erase pain. You meet it.

One case centered on a house abandoned after a domestic violence tragedy. The buyer didn't pretend nothing happened. He invited spiritual advisors. Hosted block-wide design forums. Removed structural elements that held memory of trauma. Created a healing garden where the lawn had been. Before anyone moved in, neighbors walked through, blessed the rooms, wrote affirmations on hidden beams. The architecture changed, yes—but so did the emotional infrastructure.

There's also a recurring pattern called Community Consent as Capital. Some buyers don't have traditional financing. No great credit score. No institutional backing. Yet they move through the city with impact. Why? Because the block trusts them. One woman, unable to qualify through banks, spent six months hosting free workshops, mentoring youth, and supporting elders through document translation and contractor negotiation. When she pursued a property, five neighbors gave personal letters of support. One even helped fund her closing costs. That deal didn't rely on credit, it relied on credibility.

Across all these cases, the strategies repeat:

Listening becomes leverage. Buyers who attend community meetings and walk through neighborhoods before signing anything earn quiet authority.

Design reflects rhythm, not resale. Properties that honor history, through color, layout, and communal engagement, achieve sustainability, even when profits are modest.

Refusal births respect. Those who walk away from high-dollar offers that violate community trust become anchors for local movement.

Emotional architecture beats sterile efficiency. A home filled with local artwork, family stories, and dignity-based lease terms offers more value than a flipped investment.

One buyer even rewrote his own design framework after recording interviews with seventeen elders. Instead of open concepts, he created layered layouts that reflected privacy needs, generational use, and cultural flow. The results weren't faster, but they were fuller. The community responded with welcome. Contractors volunteered hours. Future deals followed organically, without listings or pitches.

The most powerful lesson is this: street wisdom lives in rhythm. It shows up not in profit margins, but in porch gatherings, mural dedications, and unplanned testimonials from elders. Every case is different, but the patterns persist.

You don't dominate the block with spreadsheets. You co-create with care, adjust with humility, and walk with honor. That's how you build a legacy that doesn't just exist, it teaches.

Part Five

The Blueprint Beneath The Mistakes—Failure As Structure, Not Shame

For every celebrated rehab, every block revitalization that draws applause and policy interest, there is another story, quieter, harder, more tangled. Not because it lacked vision, but because the street taught lessons that no classroom prepared. These stories matter because they reveal something bigger than profit: failure doesn't destroy a mission. It maps it. When documented with care and reviewed without ego, mistakes become blueprints. Not shortcuts to success, but scaffolds for rhythm that survives friction.

One such case unfolded in Memphis. A builder acquired a triplex on a block he didn't know well, a deal shaped by timing, not alignment. The property had sat vacant for six years. The seller, out of state and eager to let go, accepted a cash offer of $21,000, no inspections, no contingencies. The buyer was experienced, smart, and strategic. But this time, he skipped ritual. He didn't walk the block. Didn't knock on doors. Didn't ask what the building had held emotionally. And what the building held was resentment.

Three families had been displaced from that triplex when a predatory landlord allowed the structure to decay while collecting inflated rent. Evictions came swift. The block never forgot. So when rehab began, neighbors didn't cheer, they watched silently, their faces hard with memory. The builder noticed it too late. His signage—"Legacy Living Memphis"—was received as irony.

The mistakes compounded:

The rehab team installed security cameras and motion lights without community input, sparking rumors of surveillance.

The flooring style used synthetic panels that residents said reminded them of prison interiors.

Lease terms were designed with flexibility for turnover, but residents wanted permanence, not rotation.

Halfway through the project, tension erupted. Graffiti was tagged on the side wall: "Ownership without honor is theft."

The builder paused everything.

He convened neighbors. Not a marketing meeting—but a truth session. He sat with twenty residents and asked, "What did I miss?"

They answered.

"You missed the pain."

"You missed the ritual."

"You missed the memory."

And most clearly: "We don't want a building. We want belonging."

From that session came a pivot that rewrote the future of the project.

The builder restructured one unit entirely, not as a rental, but as a community anchor space. It became a rotating hub for storytelling, youth education, and tenant advocacy workshops. He commissioned local artists to design murals representing block history, placed inside each stairwell. Lease agreements were rewritten in collaboration with neighborhood leaders, including clauses that honored cultural continuity, like requiring shared outdoor space programming and block engagement hours per year.

Financial impact? Immediate setback. Rehab costs increased by $12,000. Profit margins shrunk. Timeline stretched three more months.

Emotional impact? Transformation.

Neighbors began gathering on the porch again. Youth hosted a back-to-school event in the anchor unit. Two elders joined the advisory circle for other renters. The once-watchful silence broke into ritual.

That project didn't heal everything. But it shifted the energy. And more importantly, it produced documentation. The builder wrote a 22-page internal report titled "The Project That Re-taught Me Presence." In it, he created a checklist for future acquisitions:

1. Walk the block at least three times before signing.

2. Interview at least three residents about property history.

3. Present the rehab plan to neighbors before permits are filed.

4. Include visual and narrative elements that reflect legacy, not aesthetics.

5. Build a community adjustment clause into lease agreements.

This report became required reading for his team. It now lives inside his company's onboarding packet. New hires don't begin with strategy, they begin with repentance.

Another blueprint grew from an entirely different error: overconfidence in cultural translation.

In Philadelphia, a young developer tried to replicate a successful real estate model from her hometown, a "shared stair" concept that built inter-unit community through open design. It had worked beautifully in her original city, where blocks were shaped by cooperative rhythms. But in this new neighborhood, where privacy was sacred due to years of surveillance, open stairs felt invasive.

The feedback came quickly. Tenants expressed discomfort. Visitors felt exposed. One resident left prematurely, saying, "This place is architecturally stunning but emotionally wrong."

The developer didn't hide the failure. She redesigned the stairwell. Built partitions. Incorporated visual privacy cues, layered curtains, switchable glass, noise buffers. She published the process. Released an article titled "Design Can't Be Duplicated Across Memory Maps." That article traveled through real estate circles and cultural preservation forums. She became known not for being perfect, but for being present.

That failure shaped her next model: before any blueprint, she now hosts what she calls "Memory Mapping Circles." Residents gather to share spatial needs, emotional boundaries, communal preferences. No design begins until those stories surface. That pivot didn't happen because she had the right theory, it happened because she honored the correction.

These stories repeat across cities:

A Chicago buyer misjudges noise levels and installs standard windows—then redoes everything with double-seal glass and blackout filters after neighborhood protests.

A Dallas builder selects premium modern siding, only to discover it symbolically clashes with local heritage narratives. He replaces it with reclaimed barnwood donated by community elders.

A Baltimore rehabber assumes demand for multi-unit living, then transforms an apartment into a wellness studio after learning the block needed mental health space more than extra bedrooms.

Each of these failures maps a lesson. Not just in design. Not just in strategy. But in street wisdom.

You don't build real estate with perfection. You build it with rhythm. With correction. With remembrance. You document your losses. You publish your pivots. You speak about your misalignments with honesty. And in doing so, your truth becomes someone else's prevention. Your humility becomes someone else's clarity.

The blueprint beneath the mistake is the most valuable artifact you have. Because it teaches without applause. It reshapes without ego. It shows what presence looks like when pressure tries to override purpose.

Part Six

Shared Ownership, Block Collaboration, And The Rise Of Collective Equity

There comes a point in every ownership journey where the vision outgrows the blueprint. Not because the building is too small, but because the movement becomes too expansive. One rehab inspires another. One lease rewrites expectations. One mural reframes memory. And suddenly, the work is no longer about a single buyer or property. It becomes collaboration. Shared ownership. The street starts teaching a deeper rhythm: equity isn't just individual, it's collective. That's when the real transformation begins.

This part of the chapter unpacks the evolution from singular restoration to communal creation. Not theory. Not models made in boardrooms. Real blocks. Real families. Real frameworks born from necessity, culture, and repetition.

Start in Newark, where three women, all with different backgrounds in education, finance, and design, decided not to build alone. Each had tried, separately, to rehab properties in marginalized areas. Each had faced city resistance, contractor failures, and community disconnect. So they merged, not as a company, but as a legacy cooperative. They pooled capital, shared mentorship notes, split contacts. And most importantly, they created a block charter, a document outlining how decisions would be made, how cultural respect would be maintained, and how profit would be reinvested.

Their model wasn't immediate. The first joint purchase floundered when a lien was discovered post-acquisition. They pivoted, using one member's credit to refinance, another's family ties to negotiate reduction, and the third's legal education to challenge documentation flaws. That pivot would've collapsed a solo effort. But together, they moved.

The rehab that followed changed everything. The property became a shared-use structure: one unit for stable rental, one unit for youth programming, one unit for live-in legacy stewardship. Each woman rotated presence quarterly. Tenants weren't just renters, they were participants in a rhythm. Lease agreements included community engagement requirements. Design decisions were made collaboratively. Murals were proposed and voted on by residents and block elders.

Profit? Modest. Impact? Monumental.

Within a year:

Two surrounding homeowners approached the trio about cooperative ownership of vacant lots.

A city council member cited their model during a zoning equity hearing.

A youth tenant created a podcast titled "Three Women, One Block, Many Lessons," now studied in local colleges.

A mutual aid pantry opened in the refurbished garage.

Street wisdom teaches: shared ownership isn't dilution, it's multiplication.

Now move to Charlotte, where five families decided they'd had enough of the cycle: rent, displacement, silence. They chose to buy land together, not because they had cash, but because they had each other. One family had saved $9,000.

Another had building experience. Two had credit stability. The fifth had a history of zoning law study. They formed a community equity circle, purchased a distressed property for $41,000, and documented every step, not just in spreadsheets, but in journaling, prayer rituals, oral history recordings.

Their goals were simple: shared housing, stabilized legacy, and communal wealth. Each family occupied one floor. Shared spaces were co-designed. Conflict resolution protocols were written and practiced. They created a rotation for stewardship tasks: repairs, budgeting, mentorship. When one family faced job loss, the others voted to adjust the financial framework, not out of charity,but out of rhythm.

The city tried to challenge their model, calling it "unconventional tenancy." The group responded with documentation, public forums, and social media storytelling. Their movement gathered support. Housing rights advocates stepped in. Urban planners requested interviews.

One year later:

The property was classified as "multi-residential with cultural variance protection."

Their cooperative received a grant to host neighborhood design workshops.

Three elders gifted surrounding land parcels to the group's future community trust.

A local university partnered to document the model as a case study in equitable development.

Lessons echoed:

When ownership is shared with intention, accountability becomes culture, not compliance.

Collaborative design reflects multiple truths, reducing blind spots and increasing belonging.

Shared risk produces deeper resilience.

Legacy becomes collective memory, maintained by rituals, not just records.

There's also the story of unspoken collaboration, where ownership remains individual, but rhythm aligns.

In Kansas City, seven solo buyers rehabilitated adjacent properties. At first, they worked in silos. But as tensions emerged, trash overflow, contractor overlap, youth programming disconnect, they created a Block Stewardship Guild. It wasn't legal. It wasn't formal. But it lived.

Each buyer agreed to host one neighborhood event per season. They shared vetted vendor lists. If one property faced emergency repair, others contributed labor or funds. Property taxes were monitored collectively. The group even created a block newsletter: real estate updates mixed with cultural pieces, elder interviews, and youth voices.

The collaboration birthed outcomes far beyond what was imagined:

Crime rates decreased.

Maintenance costs stabilized.

A city grant was awarded based on "block cohesion metrics."

One rehabbed porch became the community's unofficial meeting space.

No one sacrificed ownership. They expanded it. Street wisdom teaches: you can hold a deed and still share rhythm. That's ownership without isolation.

Perhaps the most powerful example came from a Detroit neighborhood where no single buyer had emerged, but where collaborative caretaking had taken root.

The residents began treating vacant homes as community canvases, not to gentrify, but to reimagine. They painted messages of hope, memory, resistance. They sealed roofs not with city approval, but with pooled resources and volunteer labor. They created a map of vacant parcels, documenting stories tied to each one. And when a developer arrived trying to acquire land for commercial use, the community responded,not with protest, but with narrative. They produced a pamphlet titled "These Blocks Breathe", handed it to the zoning committee, and won the right to create a land trust.

No investor led the charge. No legal entity built the frame. Just people. With rhythm. With wisdom.

And that pamphlet?

It traveled far. Urban planning circles. Real estate forums. Public policy symposiums. One woman said, "This paper changed how I walk into property deals now." Another said, "I show this to every funder before I speak." Because legacy isn't always built with hammers. Sometimes it's built with memory.

Street wisdom teaches that ownership done alone can stabilize a home. But ownership done together can stabilize a future.

Part Seven

Generational Transfer And Emotional Wealth—How Wisdom Becomes The Real Estate

Ownership isn't just about what you acquire, it's about what you pass. Not just the buildings, but the blueprints. Not just the deeds, but the decisions. Street wisdom reaches its highest form when knowledge becomes legacy. When homes pass from hand to hand, heart to heart, not just with paperwork, but with emotional contracts that guide the next generation through clarity, context, and commitment. That's where real estate leaves the land and enters the spirit.

It begins with a truth: many of us were never taught what it means to inherit with structure. Properties changed hands through grief, confusion, whispered expectations, or sudden silence. Grandmother died, and the house became a mystery. Uncle went missing, and the title never got transferred. Cousins debated next steps while the roof caved in. These are not failures, they are reflections of systems designed to hide the playbook from communities historically excluded from equity literacy. So the process of real estate generational transfer must start with re-education. And then emotional restoration.

One case in Birmingham demonstrates the weight of emotional wealth. A grandmother had held a duplex since the 1970s, paid off, preserved, but never updated. She lived in one side, rented the other to a family friend at a reduced rate. When she passed, the property was legally inherited by three grandchildren. But emotionally, the structure was sacred ground. Birthdays, block cookouts, neighborhood watch meetings, all had taken place under that roof. The heirs froze. They didn't want to sell. Didn't want to renovate. Didn't want to touch anything. But time was moving. Pipes failed. Rent stopped flowing. Grief turned into decay.

Then one grandchild stepped forward,not with authority, but with alignment. She proposed something rare: not a renovation plan, but a legacy stewardship circle. She gathered the family. They began narrating memories. They mapped which rooms meant what. They wrote down her grandmother's phrases. They created a "Values Manifesto" that outlined the spiritual rules of the home. Rule one: rent must reflect dignity. Rule two: design must echo ancestral style. Rule three: the home is not just income, it's impact.

From that session, they developed a generational repair model. Funds came from a local heritage preservation grant. Renovations were minimal but intentional: patching leaks, restoring flooring, fresh paint in legacy tones. They didn't erase the home, they refreshed it. Rent resumed at fair terms, with income pooled into a family legacy account. Every Thanksgiving, they met in the living room. Read the manifesto aloud. Added new lessons. That home became more than a unit to it became curriculum.

Another case unfolded in Tulsa, where a father passed his four-property portfolio to his daughter. The structures were clean. Titles were tight. But the father, a quiet man who never taught his daughter the ropes, left behind silence instead of systems. She inherited confusion: legal terms, zoning quirks, maintenance stress, tax anxiety. The properties began draining her.

She paused the rentals. Sat down with a real estate educator who specialized in legacy management. They built an emotional audit protocol. What does each property hold? What story shaped its purchase? What were the unspoken standards her father enforced? She interviewed former tenants. Documented block history. Discovered that one building had housed civil rights meetings. Another had sheltered displaced elders during winter storms.

She republished lease agreements with annotated footnotes: "This property exists in honor of those who resisted displacement." "We repair quickly here because the previous owner believed speed reflects care." "This kitchen has hosted hundreds of community meals, may it continue." Tenants responded with reverence. She received messages like "Thank you for making me part of something larger than rent."

Her portfolio became spiritual infrastructure.

Generational transfer must include documentation. Not just wills and titles, but belief maps. You create a "Legacy Packet" for each property. It includes:

Ownership philosophy

Emotional architecture notes

Design logic

Maintenance rhythm

Community impact records

Letters to future stewards

This packet becomes the anchor. Whether your child inherits it or your mentee does, they know the why, not just the what.

Some choose ritual handoff events. When transferring property, they host family ceremonies. Blessings. Readings. Storytelling. One woman passed her duplex to her niece and wrote a speech titled "What This Porch Has Seen." She read it aloud as neighbors watched. That speech now hangs in the entryway. Future generations will walk past it daily. That's legacy preserved.

Emotional contracts aren't legal, but they are binding. You say: "This home will never be rented without honoring elder memory." Or "This property must host a healing ritual annually." These expectations may seem abstract, but they guide decision-making. They protect soul from dilution.

Documentation also includes mistakes. You write the chapter titled "What I Would've Done Differently." It includes stories of deals taken too fast. Contracts accepted too loosely. Rehab rushed too brutally. And you annotate the lessons. Your inheritor reads those and feels not shame, but inheritance of resilience.

Street wisdom says: your true wealth is what you hand off when you're no longer holding the hammer.

In Atlanta, one block created a collective legacy trust. Five families combined their properties. They each contributed written history, spiritual expectations, and community goals. The trust operates not through legal rigidity but through relationship practice. Each family names a youth steward. The stewards meet quarterly. They discuss what's working.

What's shifting. They read aloud stories of block resistance and renewal.

A mural on the side of one home reads: "Legacy isn't passed. It's practiced."

Real estate schools rarely teach emotional wealth. But every home that outlasts its builder proves: it's the emotion, not the architecture, that carries forward.

You don't just transfer title.
You transfer wisdom.
You don't just pass equity.
You pass rhythm.
You don't just gift buildings.
You gift belief systems.

Final Part

Integrated Legacy—How Past Moves, Present Presence, And Future Rhythm Shape Stability

Legacy isn't a moment. It's a movement braided from memory, mastery, and momentum. The street doesn't just offer isolated lessons, it delivers patterns that, when studied and synthesized, shape durable frameworks for community stability. And now, with case studies unpacked, mistakes redeemed, deals refined, and ownership expanded, we arrive at the culmination: how to integrate all of it. Not with formulas, but with rhythm logic. This final section ties past decisions, present presence, and future direction into a unified strategy, one that honors ancestry, corrects architecture, uplifts culture, and refuses fragility.

At the heart of integration lies rhythmic continuity. This means every property, every partnership, and every process carries a core theme. Your first rehab in 2014? It used salvaged doors from a neighborhood school. Your second rehab? It echoed that story in its porch design, even though the layout was different. Your third property, used for financial literacy workshops? It featured mural art telling the origin myth of your first deal. That's not branding, that's belief with continuity. People start to recognize your work before they know your name. Elders say, "That looks like one of yours." And youth begin tracing patterns through photos, knowing this work belongs to a larger purpose.

Integration means your past mistakes are made visible and structural. Instead of hiding your missteps, you document them in your workflows, curriculum, and mentorship tools. A collapsed roof due to budget mismanagement becomes a module in your ownership course. A community misalignment you caused by ignoring elder consultation gets memorialized in your design ritual checklist. One Baltimore builder created a gallery titled "Rooms We Rebuilt Twice" each photo displayed a version of failure turned into wisdom. That kind of humility doesn't weaken a legacy, it bulletproofs it. When people study your process, they don't see ego. They see evolution.

Present presence is where your real power lives. Legacy isn't built from abstract principles, it's carried through how you move today. How you speak at block meetings. How you write lease agreements with clarity and care. How you narrate your decisions in plain, powerful language. One of the sharpest builders in Oakland began publishing decision diaries, monthly reflections on what she chose, what she rejected, and why. No self-congratulation. Just transparency. Her audience grew beyond real estate into policy makers, educators, and activists. People realized her method was more than structure, it was strategy grounded in soul.

Another builder reframed the inspection process not as a technical step but as a community ritual. Instead of sending contractors alone, he invited block leaders to walk with him. They spoke about air flow, safety, ancestral symbolism, and local history. The inspection report included footnotes from neighbors. That integration of technical and cultural feedback made the city take notice and sparked a new guideline template that dozens now use.

Future rhythm is shaped by continuity through collective practice. Integration means you teach your successors not just skills, but sequencing. You show them how your deals map across time: what you learned from your first purchase that shaped your third rehab, and what you refused in your fifth negotiation because your second partnership taught you the cost of dilution. It's not about legacy as static artifact, it's legacy as dynamic motion.

This rhythm gets built into communal documentation frameworks. You host workshops on story-based zoning analysis, block engagement mapping, and trauma-aware rehab. You publish guides, not with jargon, but with poetry and policy braided together. One publishing cooperative created The Rhythm Reader, a field manual with annotated photos, lineage-focused lease templates, repair rituals, and value-led vendor contracts. It's been cited in academic journals, real estate forums, and city council hearings. That's integration at work: your lessons don't live in your head. They live in the hands of others.

Integrated legacy must also include resilience architecture. This means your properties are not designed to withstand only weather, but systems. Economic shifts, policy attacks, exploitation attempts. You write lease clauses that protect against displacement, and you teach tenants what each clause means. You build emergency repair protocols and neighborhood alert networks. You don't wait for city support, you design survival strategy from the block up. When others falter, your community holds together not by accident, but by architecture.

One block in Richmond adopted a multi-home covenant: five separate owners agreed to shared protocols, eviction resistance, vendor monitoring, and local youth employment guarantees. Each property displayed an emblem: a small carved stone in the garden engraved with "We Hold Each Other." That kind of resilience isn't corporate, it's cultural. It's designed into the rhythm, baked into the branding, and practiced as daily presence.

Integration also means ceremonial consistency. You don't let tradition fade between deals. Every time you acquire a property, you host a blessing. Every rehab finishes with a block walk, not just for showcase, but for sharing lessons learned. Every lease begins with a reading, not just of terms, but of testimony. That repetition turns real estate into ritual. And ritual builds memory that lives longer than any spreadsheet.

You create a legacy grid, a map that visualizes your values across time. It connects your properties, partners, educational materials, mural commissions, advisory roles, and spiritual practices. You annotate it annually. You teach others to map theirs. This tool becomes not just analysis, but affirmation. You see the work move. You see its texture. You understand not just what you've built, but what you've shifted.

Finally, you design a stewardship circle, a group of people empowered to carry your methods forward. Not just when you retire, but while you still build. You name this circle publicly. You publish their roles. You mentor them not with lectures, but with collaboration. One Chicago leader named her circle The Rhythm Weavers, and each month, they co-create blueprints, review contracts, and host healing sessions for new rehabbers. That structure ensures your legacy isn't just remembered, it's remixed.

Because integration is not about control, it's about expansion with clarity. Your legacy must outlive your leadership. Your rhythm must echo beyond your body. And your wisdom must become part of a community's infrastructure, not just its memory.

Every case study, every deal, every mistake, every mural, every lease, every refusal, braids into this framework. Integrated legacy means you stop building for applause. You start building for permanence. And every time someone walks past your work and says, "That feels like care," you know you didn't just own property.

You built stability.

You became rhythm.

You made memory the method.

CHAPTER TWELVE

BURN THE MORTGAGE—BUILD THE LEGACY

Part One

The Last Payment Is Not The Last Lesson

The final payment clears. The balance drops to zero. You hold the deed without a monthly reminder. And while many call that freedom, you call it formation. Because burning the mortgage is not just symbolic, it's strategic. It marks the shift from survival-based ownership to legacy-based stewardship. From contractual compliance to generational curriculum. Real estate stops being reactive. It becomes ritual. And now, as the dust clears and the checkbook rests, you begin the true work: building systems of value that outlast your name.

But first, pause the celebration. Not to dull the joy, but to deepen the reflection. Because ownership, as it stands in most narratives, ends with debt elimination. "You made it." "Congratulations, you're free." But legacy asks for more than liberation, it demands construction. The deed in your hand is not the trophy. It's the textbook.

Burning the mortgage must be accompanied by story-based documentation. You start by writing how you paid it down, not just the numbers, but the strategies. The months where rent almost missed. The pivot to short-term rental. The repairs handled through sweat equity and block labor. You create a timeline that includes not only transactions, but emotional decisions. You annotate each year with lessons learned, rituals introduced, relationships formed. The home didn't just house you, it healed you, stretched you, taught you. That wisdom must be preserved.

This begins the crafting of your Ownership Ethos Packet, a legacy binder or digital archive filled not with technicality, but transparency. It holds:

Your philosophy of stewardship

Your maintenance rhythms and repair rituals

Your budgeting pivots and financial literacy practices

Your emotional mapping of each room and its purpose

Letters to future stewards explaining decisions made

Family stories tied to each square foot

The packet becomes curriculum. Not just for heirs, but for mentees, partners, future builders. Because generational wisdom must live beyond your wallet.

You also revisit your space rituals. Now that debt no longer guides the calendar, you redesign how the home engages the people inside it. You host reflection dinners in the backyard, asking each guest to share a memory shaped by the property. You install a wall for intergenerational dreams, notes added monthly by residents and visitors alike. You open the porch for youth study sessions or elder oral history circles. This isn't hospitality. This is architectural affirmation. The home speaks not just of freedom, but of philosophy.

With the mortgage gone, your equity becomes mobility, not just financial, but strategic. You can refinance for purpose, not panic. You can transfer value without triggering instability. You begin to explore community gifting mechanics. Can you lend your home to emerging entrepreneurs for pop-up workshops? Can you host block planning sessions? Can your home function as a rhythm space for movements larger than your own? You move beyond residency. You begin rotation.

But legacy also requires emotional clarity with heirs. You gather the family, not just to announce deed status, but to outline vision. You say, "This is not just your inheritance. It's your responsibility." You speak about stewardship standards. You walk them through the packet. You discuss possibilities: co-ownership, rental with dignity, transformation into trust. You let the conversation breathe. You include disagreement. You facilitate values-aligned decision-making. Because passing down knowledge means passing down capacity.

Some builders create a legacy codex, a written or visual system that defines what the home must protect. For example:

"This home must never be rented above affordability thresholds for this block."

"This yard must host at least one community event per year."

"This kitchen is a memory chamber. Cooking here must reflect ancestral practice."

"This garage will always remain available for youth programming."

These codex entries operate as spiritual infrastructure. Not legally binding, but emotionally sacred. They shape how future stewards interpret the property. They prevent drift. They hold rhythm.

Financial value becomes relational instruction. You don't just tell heirs what the home is worth. You explain how to negotiate equity without exploitation. You teach them how to evaluate buyers, investors, funders. You demonstrate legacy leverage, how to say no to inflated offers that disrespect history. You role-play contract reviews. You annotate sample listings with commentary. That's more than mentorship. That's armor.

You also model block stewardship systems. You show how the home connects to the wider rhythm. How sidewalks matter. How neighbors form the firewall against displacement. You draft templates for block involvement: newsletters, cleanup rotations, zoning advocacy letters. You equip your successors not just to manage a house, but to manage community continuity.

Perhaps most crucially, you build a memory transfer process. Not just stories told over dinner, but documented, curated, housed. A digital archive of repair decisions, funding sources, mistakes made, forgiveness offered. One room becomes a memory library. One drawer holds ritual objects from past milestones. One shelf displays printed contracts annotated with lessons. The structure becomes pedagogy. The building becomes book.

And finally, you design your legacy ceremony. A public ritual where you declare the mortgage burned, the knowledge preserved, the system alive. You don't just say thank you. You say: this is how we build now. You invite mentees, elders, community partners. You unveil the packet. You read your codex. You light a flame, not of destruction, but of instruction.

Because burning the mortgage is not the end of ownership, it's the beginning of stewardship that teaches, transforms, and transcends.

Part Two

Systems Of Value—Designing Inheritance That Teaches, Heals, And Empowers

When the mortgage burns, what's left must be more than bricks and title. What remains must move, teach, protect, and guide. Legacy is not the house, it's the system you build around it. And that system must carry cultural wisdom, financial resilience, emotional clarity, and structural intention. This part of the chapter unpacks how to create frameworks that speak louder than the deed, how to pass down knowledge that functions like architecture: layered, load-bearing, and weatherproof across generations.

Legacy systems begin with succession clarity. You don't just list beneficiaries. You narrate stewardship. This means outlining who will hold the property, but also who will hold its rhythm. You write a family charter: not just who owns what, but how decisions get made. Include roles, maintenance coordinator, community liaison, financial overseer, historian. Rotate annually. Build mentorship into each role. This distributes authority and sustains accountability.

Next, design your emotional inheritance protocol. Every home passes memory. The question is whether memory will arrive curated or chaotic. You build curation. This includes audio recordings of past experiences. Photographs annotated with stories. Ritual instructions for events like the anniversary of ownership or community history month. You create a memory map, assigning meaning to rooms, corners, thresholds. Future generations walk through not just space, but significance.

Financial inheritance must include access logic. Not just value, but velocity. You document how equity should be used, with examples of good and bad options. One builder created a chart titled "If You Tap The Equity..." with three columns:

Values-aligned uses: Block rehab, youth tuition, community fund contribution

Neutral uses: Travel, upgrades, small business investment

Misaligned uses: Exploitative flipping, luxury purchases without community benefit, silent partnerships with displacement-linked developers

That chart lives in the legacy binder, revisited each year. It doesn't control, it teaches. You also provide sample budget plans, capital request forms, and an annual financial literacy tradition: the family holds a wealth strategy weekend with speakers, workshops, and scenario case studies. The home becomes school.

Design your cultural succession model. Ownership without identity is erosion. You ensure that future stewards retain memory of place, people, and mission. You build cultural contracts, written agreements that say: "This home will always reflect our roots." That may mean preserving colors, textures, floorplans, language, or block relationships. You assign a cultural archivist in the family. That person maintains legacy items, facilitates storytelling sessions, and updates historical records.

To avoid power hoarding, create intergenerational councils. One builder created The Legacy Council: three elders, two middle generation leaders, and two youth. They meet quarterly to vote on big decisions, renovation shifts, property use, community partnerships. Every voice matters. Every vote is shaped by ritual: the council begins each meeting with a reading from the original ownership ethos packet. This rhythm ensures continuity. It also prevents drift.

The system must include educational transference. You teach heirs how to build, not just how to inherit. Create content: narrated walkthroughs of past deals. Annotated contracts with commentary. Block relationship maps that explain the difference between presence and performance. You design property-based curriculum: maintenance manuals written like storybooks. Lease agreement templates featuring footnotes on emotional intention. These tools make knowledge tangible. Future stewards aren't left with overwhelm. They're handed playbooks.

Preserve systemic integrity through shared access frameworks. You define how the property is used for external impact. Schedule windows for community programming. Design income-sharing systems for partnerships. Include clauses that prevent exclusive access. One family inserted a "Community Continuity Clause": any future renovation must be presented to block elders and align with stewardship goals. That clause has prevented displacement-linked rental models. Integration protects alignment.

Your legacy system should also manage ritual and rhythm. Outline key ceremonies: Ownership Anniversary, Founder's Day, Stewardship Shifts. Create scripts for each. Publish them. Encourage others to adapt them for their homes. A New Orleans builder wrote The Rhythm Ritual Book, a 40-page guide featuring instructions for blessing thresholds, dedicating rooms, and honoring ancestors with each season shift. That book now lives in over 300 community households.

To safeguard emotional wealth, design protection circles. A group of trusted advisors, not just financial, but emotional and cultural, who assess property use, partner engagement, and rhythm integrity. They meet semi-annually. Review stewardship notes. Evaluate block impact. Recommend course correction when needed. These circles prevent misalignment and offer communal correction without condemnation.

You also build inheritance of presence. When heirs receive the property, they also receive commitments: community relationship hours, block advocacy tasks, annual reporting. That may include hosting listening circles or attending zoning hearings. Legacy lives not in possession, but in participation. The system ensures that each steward remains visible, active, and aligned.

Finally, document your legacy closure protocols. If ever the property must be sold, you outline how. To whom. Under what terms. One builder created a "Ritual Sale Plan" which included farewell ceremonies, community debrief sessions, a published transition report, and a legacy preservation archive to remain on site. Even in exit, the system speaks.

Because real legacy doesn't reside in ownership. It lives in systems.

Systems that teach. Heal. Protect. Evolve.

Systems of value, beyond profit.

Part Three

Make Legacy Visible—Design, Publish, And Protect The Message In Motion

Legacy does not whisper, it radiates. When real estate evolves into rhythm, when ownership becomes stewardship, when memory transforms into infrastructure, the final imperative is clarity. To make the movement visible. Not performative visibility. Not trend-chasing exposure. But curated presence. Cultural clarity. Visual truth. Publishing legacy is not a branding exercise, it's a responsibility. Your values must be seen, understood, shared, and protected. Otherwise, they risk dilution in the generations ahead.

This begins with visual coherence across every artifact of ownership. Your property signage, social documentation, archival materials, and educational tools must reflect the same design logic. Choose a palette rooted in culture, not commerce. Maybe burnt orange from ancestral soil. Maybe deep indigo from block murals. Each color symbolizes more than aesthetics, it references legacy. Select typography with tone: a font with weight and curvature to match the emotional intelligence of your message. Your design kit becomes the heartbeat of the movement, used across newsletters, community invitations, stewardship packets, and ritual programs.

But visual language alone isn't enough. The message must be published across formats with intentional cadence. This means monthly reflection letters to your community partners. Quarterly rhythm reports detailing stewardship shifts, lessons learned, and block updates. A digital archive housing annotated blueprints, past renovation strategies, and negotiation debriefs. You host a podcast, not to entertain, but to teach. Each episode unpacks a decision. You narrate the week your contractor ghosted mid-job, and what you did next. You discuss why you said no to an investor offering double your asking price. These stories are legacy-in-motion. They allow others to learn without risking their own.

You also publish your ownership philosophies through creative media. That might be a visual journal, photographs accompanied by handwritten captions about ritual and rhythm. A short film featuring block voices explaining how the property impacted memory. A spoken word series performed inside the home. These media pieces are not marketing, they're messaging. Their audience includes future stewards, block historians, city planners, and young leaders with no blueprint. By documenting with rhythm, you build emotional infrastructure others can inherit.

Your publishing strategy must include a visible ownership framework. You create a Legacy Operating Manual: a document explaining the philosophy behind financial decisions, repair logic, event programming, and community engagement. It includes annotated leases, decision maps, values statements, block story transcripts, and design justifications. Each section is published with footnotes referencing past mistakes, context about culture, and examples of what success looks like beyond spreadsheets. That manual must be accessible, not locked behind intellectual gatekeeping, but formatted for clarity. Shared in print, audio, and visual form. Open-source presence as pedagogy.

Visibility also requires public ceremony as education. You host gatherings not just for celebration, but for curriculum. These may be ritual dinners where each course reflects a stage of the ownership journey. Or porch salons where elders discuss block history. Or public walk-throughs with future buyers, narrating the emotional logic behind design choices. Visibility is practice. When presence becomes habit, the community begins to co-teach the message. Your legacy moves without you speaking. That's when rhythm becomes public record.

You build a memory museum within the home itself. This isn't a room of nostalgia, it's a living archive. The walls hold past floor plans annotated with feedback loops. Shelves carry repair logs alongside photographs of each phase. One corner includes community letters written during zoning conflicts. Another holds a ledger of every gift the property received: volunteer hours, donated materials, mentorship circles. That museum is accessible. Tenants use it. Visitors contribute to it. Future owners study it. Presence as permanence.

You also establish a publishing imprint for real estate rhythm work. This isn't just your brand. It's a collective movement channel. Others contribute: mentorship reflections, community essays, architectural meditations, cultural contracts. The imprint produces journals, anthologies, toolkits, and policy suggestions. It becomes a distribution engine for rhythm-aligned knowledge, created by people who refuse mainstream frameworks. Publishing isn't performance. It's resistance against forgetting.

Protecting visibility includes legal and ethical defense mechanisms. Trademark your symbolism, not to gatekeep, but to prevent dilution. Write attribution guidelines for your materials. Create citation protocols for your frameworks. Share your story widely, but include disclaimers about context and cultural specificity. You don't want imitation, you want adaptation with accountability. Build a network of trusted collaborators who monitor usage. When your legacy is referenced, they ensure rhythm remains intact.

Visibility must be sustained through intergenerational media rhythm. You train future stewards to create monthly updates. They write blog posts, record reflections, host community photo sessions. They track changes, publish notes, invite questions. Legacy doesn't expire, it evolves. By building publishing into their responsibility, you ensure rhythm breathes past your leadership.

Finally, you invest in cultural modeling platforms. These include neighborhood installations explaining your ownership methodology. Curriculum partnerships with schools to teach rhythm-based real estate. Civic dialogues using your work as case study. You become a reference point for how legacy lives. Not because you're famous, but because your visibility educates.

Real estate doesn't teach. You teach.

Ownership doesn't inspire. You inspire.

Legacy isn't what you keep, it's what you curate, publish, and protect.

Part Four

From Ashes To Architecture—How Ownership Transforms Into Cultural Infrastructure

Once the mortgage is gone and the deed stands clean, the real work of legacy begins, not in finality, but in formation. What has been paid off through years of negotiation, sweat equity, community engagement, and strategic discipline must now be repurposed into systems that move, teach, protect, and evolve. The home transitions from shelter to structure, from an individual triumph to an intergenerational framework. It begins serving as infrastructure: cultural, emotional, instructional, and ideological.

Architectural identity must be imbued with meaning. Properties that remain static lose their ability to transmit values. Each room carries function, but must also carry symbolic intention. A hallway reflects continuity across generations. A dining room hosts the embodiment of intergenerational strategy. The porch becomes a place not merely for welcome, but for neighborhood vigilance and relational exchange. These intentions are not left unspoken. They are documented, taught, and built into rituals, signage, and community practice.

Ownership philosophy takes form through documentation. A personal manifesto outlines decisions made, pivots taken, lessons absorbed, and relationships honored through the stewardship process. Published in full, distributed internally, housed visibly within the home, and used during family convenings, this document transcends legal language to operate as spiritual infrastructure. It narrates the purpose behind each architectural choice and policy design, giving the building depth beyond function.

Seasonal rhythm mapping ensures continuity of ritual. Ownership is maintained through cycles. A legacy home requires a ceremonial calendar: planting rituals in spring, mentorship programming in summer, archival review in autumn, spiritual restoration in winter. Ritual transforms architecture into narrative. Properties no longer stand idle, they breathe.

The stewardship curriculum evolves into a full legacy toolkit. This includes annotated leases, repair logs, oral history files, annotated floor plans, negotiation debriefs, and community engagement workflows. Each component not only educates, it preserves the decisions that shaped presence. Format varies depending on the community: print, digital platform, audio reflections, and video walkthroughs. Story-based learning replaces abstract instruction. Knowledge is narrated through lived experience.

Legacy design is embedded in the structure of the home through a permanent archive. Photos, documents, receipts, letters, annotated repair contracts, zoning advocacy artifacts, and community correspondence live inside a curated section of the property. It's not hidden, it's integrated into public or family-accessible rooms. The archive invites interaction and updates. It is reviewed annually. It becomes curriculum in practice.

Ownership is expanded through stewardship councils, intergenerational, multi-voiced groups that maintain alignment. These councils review community impact, property usage, partnership decisions, and ceremony planning. Members rotate through assigned roles with mentorship protocol. The rhythm of the home is not kept by one steward alone, it is held collectively, through relational trust and documented practice.

A ritual transfer protocol is structured in advance. Not just for inheritance, but for all forms of transition. This protocol outlines emotional closure events, community dialogues, transparency reporting, and cultural preservation mandates. If property is transferred, sold, or repositioned, the rhythm is retained through archived legacy packets, creative content preservation, and block-based celebration. Transition is coordinated, not abrupt.

Community integration is mapped. The property's function within the ecosystem of the block, schools, local businesses, cultural institutions, faith spaces, and civic structures, is diagrammed and published. This visual record is accessible, framed within the property, and updated periodically. The map operates as a spatial accountability document, encouraging continued alignment with neighborhood purpose and relational engagement.

Ethical protection frameworks support legacy integrity. These include published attribution guidelines for storytelling, symbolic protection of design choices, and community review of external representation. Symbolism is trademarked to preserve intention. Cultural contracts define how materials or frameworks may be referenced or adapted. The stewardship circle maintains oversight and advises on correction when alignment is jeopardized.

Legacy rhythm is continued through media rhythm. Future stewards are equipped and required to publish regular documentation: updates, reflections, annotated decisions, community stories, and pattern debriefs. Publishing is embedded within the stewardship process, not as vanity but as pedagogical visibility. It ensures continuation of methodology without reliance on oral assumption or memory distortion.

Community-scale modeling emerges naturally. Properties become reference points for curriculum design, block-wide stewardship mapping, advocacy training, and architectural apprenticeship. Relationships with educational institutions, media platforms, policy organizations, and cultural networks grow organically. Legacy is broadcast without performance, by virtue of presence, not publicity.

Ownership continues only if memory is maintained, structure is narrated, and decisions are passed down as systems. Homes cease to be static investments and become dynamic pedagogical structures. Each payment made, repair completed, conflict resolved, and ritual practiced is captured and added to the archive of rhythm.

The mortgage once dictated motion. Now legacy determines structure. Payment transforms into pedagogy. Ritual becomes record. Decision becomes design. Ownership becomes rhythm.

Part Five

Community Inheritance—Embedding The Rhythm Beyond The Home

Ownership refined through rhythm must be extended, made collective, embedded into the neighborhood's emotional and cultural infrastructure. A home paid in full becomes more than personal equity, it transforms into shared presence, a blueprint that lives across addresses, ages, and agendas. This transition requires deliberate integration. Not through speeches or symbolism alone, but through action systems that allow community members to inherit rhythm, not just witness it.

Begin with the property's reconfiguration into a communal learning site. Even if still privately held, the home's operations serve public pedagogy. Key rooms are used for rhythm workshops, floorplan design seminars, equity training, intergenerational storytelling. Hallways host annotated process boards detailing previous repairs. The living room becomes a documentation lab, where emerging builders study how decisions were made, why timelines shifted, and how rhythm was preserved despite pressure. Presence becomes education without posturing.

Community partners are assigned stewardship adjacents, roles that mirror home functions but activate block-wide engagement. The person coordinating porch storytelling also assists with memory curation for other legacy households. The youth hosting gardening days in the backyard co-develop seasonal rituals for community spaces. The rhythm doesn't live in the house, it moves through it, touching everything nearby. Each role includes accountability measures: monthly check-ins, narrative reviews, and reflection memos cataloged for public reference.

To ensure sustainability, design ownership dispersal tools. Create annotated frameworks others can adopt: lease templates with rhythm clauses, repair schedules with restoration rituals, financial models that reflect dignity-based pricing. You print small packets titled "The House Taught Us", each containing a single lesson, how to refuse exploitative offers, how to design without erasure, how to embed legacy in trim and tile. These packets are circulated across churches, barbershops, schools, and block meetings. Their simplicity masks their potency. Each one seeds new rhythm.

Visibility must remain honest, not ornamental. Media presence is coordinated with block narratives. When the home appears in articles or forums, community members are cited as co-authors. Their quotes appear beside design logic. Their stories shape the rhythm archive. Visibility reframes property as platform. Not to elevate one steward, but to affirm collective knowledge.

Over time, the property hosts a Rotational Residency Network. Artists, researchers, apprentice builders, policy advocates, all rotate through short stays, tasked with documenting, developing, or designing rhythm-aligned artifacts. Their work is housed onsite. Reviewed by the stewardship council. Shared publicly. These residencies inject new energy while preserving core values. The property stops being fixed in narrative. It becomes iterative memory.

Financial impact echoes through shared capital cycles. Profits generated by legacy events or curriculum sales are reinvested into block initiatives: elder repair subsidies, youth entrepreneurial grants, mural commissions, and historic signage installation. Transparency reports are published quarterly, showing how the mortgage-free status enables moral reinvestment. The numbers don't boast, they testify.

Legal reinforcement includes rhythm protection covenants. The deed is amended with clauses requiring notification if ownership changes. Conditions include community debrief sessions, cultural preservation commitments, and memory archive review. New stewards must agree not only to care for the property, but to continue its pedagogy. The rhythm remains coded into the legal structure.

The home becomes a reference point for regional rhythm systems. Leaders from other cities visit, study, replicate. Your annotated contracts, design walkthroughs, oral history templates, and stewardship rotations inform new policy drafts, curriculum modules, and block funding campaigns. Rhythm exits singularity and enters movement. Builders start naming their work in relation to yours, not out of imitation, but because your presence gave them language.

Maintenance transforms into ceremony. Each repair begins with review of the ethos packet. Volunteers write reflections. Tools are handled respectfully. Post-repair photos are captioned with testimonies: "This wall now holds our story again." "The leak was fixed with rhythm in mind." That language carries into block conversations, policy briefings, and mentorship sessions. Rhythm is spoken aloud and heard.

Documentation becomes infrastructure. Each year, stewards publish a Rhythm Review Journal, an annotated collection of what changed, what was added, what mistakes were made, what rituals expanded. The journal features block interviews, design debates, emotional check-ins, financial clarifications. It isn't promotional, it's pedagogical texture. Copies are stored onsite, circulated through block libraries, and used as curriculum in mentorship labs.

Architecture gains symbolic coding. A specific porch angle becomes known in the community as "welcome geometry." A paint blend used in restoration gets named after the matriarch who blessed the project. Children grow up identifying rhythm signals, not just as decoration, but as design logic. Those codes enter language, songs, writing. The home no longer holds culture, it extends it.

Presence adapts without dilution. As technology shifts, materials change, and block needs evolve, the home's rhythm remains intact because it is continuously re-articulated. Rituals get updated, but their values are retained. New stewards innovate while reviewing memory. Legacy never freezes, it breathes.

Part Six

Custodians Of Rhythm—Training Future Stewards To Lead With Memory And Precision

Once ownership is no longer about acquisition and defense, it becomes leadership in motion. The property becomes a proving ground, not just for design and finance, but for relational governance and value-aligned decision-making. To sustain legacy, future stewards must be trained, not in the mechanics of upkeep alone, but in the memory-based disciplines that turn property into presence. Custodians of rhythm are not figureheads. They are operators of cultural infrastructure.

Training begins with ritual orientation, a multi-day immersion designed to align emotional, ethical, and logistical expectations. New stewards enter the home not with entitlement but humility. They receive annotated walkthroughs where prior decisions are narrated with purpose. The difference between a diagonal doorway and a square one is explained not by code, but by story: "This angle was chosen to echo the entryway of the home where the founder was first taught to read." Orientation includes lessons from community members, archival readings, and simulations of zoning conflict response.

Each steward receives a Legacy Field Guide, structured as a dynamic workbook with tabs labeled Memory, Maintenance, Messaging, Mentorship, and Mistakes. For Memory, they record interviews, ritual reviews, and block history findings. Maintenance includes protocols for culturally sensitive repairs. Messaging outlines how to engage block elders, respond to media inquiries, and narrate decisions without performance. Mentorship tracks how they teach and receive knowledge. Mistakes includes required monthly reflections on errors in judgment, design missteps, or communication breakdowns. The guide is updated quarterly and reviewed by the stewardship council.

Emotional skill-building is essential. Stewards attend resilience rituals, group sessions where legacy holders from other blocks share how they navigated burnout, betrayal, loss, and comeback. These stories are documented, not as testimonials, but as warning systems. The point is not to glamorize difficulty, but to normalize recalibration. One stewardship network hosts "Monthly Missings" where participants share decisions they would undo, not out of regret, but to model rhythm recovery.

To activate cultural fluency, stewards participate in legacy language labs, sessions where they unpack neighborhood dialects, learn ceremonial phrasing, analyze historical documents for tone and metaphor, and study the ethical implications of narrative shifts. They practice saying "ownership" in a way that lands differently depending on audience, sometimes through metaphors, other times through direct spiritual linkage. These labs prevent miscommunication and deepen emotional nuance.

The program includes design interpretation clinics. Stewards do more than learn how to paint or patch. They study meaning. Why certain trim colors symbolize ancestral fire. Why porch width affects block collaboration. How sound insulation reflects respect for elder privacy. Every choice is tracked back to rhythm. Stewards complete assessments based not on code compliance, but on ability to articulate cultural consequence.

Mentorship is embedded as responsibility, not as suggestion. Stewards must recruit and train at least one junior apprentice per year. That apprentice shadows them in three phases: documentation, negotiation, and ritual hosting. Together, they publish a co-authored reflection piece outlining their evolution. This becomes part of the home archive, proof that rhythm knowledge isn't just possessed, but reproduced.

Stewardship is also tested through accountability simulations. Scenarios include a zoning challenge where block residents disagree about development, a contractor breach during cultural preservation repair, or a media request that distorts a legacy event. Stewards write, debate, and enact their responses. The council observes. Feedback is direct, not delicate. Legacy deserves precision.

Curriculum includes interdisciplinary rhythm learning. Stewards study block architecture, trauma-responsive design, spiritual ritual theory, cooperative economics, and story-centered pedagogy. Every steward must facilitate two neighborhood rhythm sessions per year. Topics range from restorative lease language to blessing murals without erasure. The home serves as classroom, commons, and archive.

Final stage of training includes a rhythm stewardship thesis, a synthesized project combining practice, documentation, and vision. Stewards write and present a proposal for the next year's legacy expansion: what part of the property will be ritualized further, how engagement will grow, what systems will be fortified. Their thesis is reviewed, revised, and then published into the property's permanent record. It's not graded, it's witnessed.

Stewardship is not a position, it's a rhythm protocol that ensures the home remains alive with presence, pedagogy, and precise care. The role rotates, but the responsibility remains fixed: preserve the meaning, evolve the systems, teach the decisions, honor the breath in the walls.

Final Part

Legacy In Circulation—Embedding Rhythm Within And Beyond The Neighborhood

Legacy cannot remain private. To endure, it must be shared, dispersed across circles of influence, embedded into the daily habits of homes, blocks, and institutions. This closing movement doesn't summarize the work, it extends it. It translates years of stewardship, ritual, and design into systems that others carry, adapt, and protect. The deed may name one owner, but the rhythm belongs to the many. And once the mortgage is burned, what's built must be bigger than equity. It must be rhythm in circulation.

Begin with rhythm repositories. These are not hard drives or locked cabinets. They are curated sites of public memory and practical teaching. One room in the home functions as a living archive, an open studio where rhythm maps, design ethics, annotated negotiation transcripts, and photographs of repair rituals are displayed. Youth walk through. Apprentices take notes. Elders point to walls saying, "That corner held our first zoning resistance meeting." These spaces transmit pedagogy through experience, not presentation.

Collaborators publish rhythm casework. Every major decision made by stewards is followed by a rhythm debrief. Not just the what, but the why and how. These case studies are distributed across block newsletters, real estate ethics courses, and policy toolkits. Each includes decision logic, alignment reviews, community reaction summaries, and annotated outcomes. The work is documented not for posterity but for practicality. Future builders don't copy, they calibrate.

Strategic rhythm gifting accelerates alignment. Stewards offer rituals, templates, methodologies, and annotated visuals to legacy-driven spaces across the region. Not as products. As possibilities. Community centers receive porch ceremony scripts. Housing cooperatives adopt dignified lease language. School art programs adapt repair blessing formats. These exchanges preserve texture while expanding reach. Rhythm is modular, not rigid.

Structures for rhythm maintenance are built into everyday governance. That means quarterly legacy reviews, stewardship council rotations, seasonal curriculum updates, and annual archiving protocols. Every practice links back to a value, from paint colors chosen with cultural memory to guest policies reflecting neighborhood healing needs. These structures don't simply organize the work, they encode the ethos.

Visual rhythm expands across the landscape. Neighborhoods begin to incorporate texture cues from the home: mural color palettes, garden layout inspiration, porch curvature principles, and signage tone. These visuals signal not trend but teaching. Passersby recognize rhythm design without needing attribution. That's visibility with values.

Knowledge dispersal is formalized through rhythm training centers. Properties host intensives: one-week immersion programs for emerging builders, cultural designers, and policy thinkers. Trainings cover community engagement alignment, restoration rituals, rhythm-based zoning navigation, and multi-generational property planning. Each participant contributes a reflection chapter to the archive. Some become mentors. Some return home and begin their own rhythm labs.

The stewardship role multiplies. No longer limited to one custodian, rhythm is carried by a network. Tenants lead ceremonies. Youth host storytelling salons. Retired neighbors consult on archive curation. Stewards facilitate, not centralize. This model ensures that rhythm doesn't rely on personality, but on shared practice.

Community rhythm impact is tracked across spheres. A living record details how many individuals engaged the systems, how many policies were influenced, how many spaces were preserved, taught, or restored. Elders narrate the data. Youth visualize it. Local press documents it. These records form the rhythm pulse report, used by organizers, educators, and builders to advocate for structural change.

Rhythm enters policy through adaptation, not confrontation. City councils quote the work. Nonprofit boards use rhythm repair logic. Developers revise impact statements based on rhythm proximity audits. Not because they were forced, but because rhythm reshaped expectation. What was once dismissed as fringe now becomes normative.

And through all of it, the property breathes. Not because it holds a title. Because it holds testimony.

It gives. It teaches. It corrects. It remembers.

No longer a house. Now a hub. A system. A ritual engine.

Legacy, once rooted in a payment, now circulates through a network of truth.

That rhythm, repeated, refined, remembered, is the architecture that outlasts any mortgage.

Now You Know

Knowledge is useless without wisdom.

SYSTEM CORRECTION WORKBOOK

REFLECTIONS ON RECLAIMING VALUE AND RESISTING EXPLOITATION

Reflection One

Breaking The Appraisal Myth

Who taught you what property was worth and what did they leave out?

Write a paragraph explaining how systemic bias shaped the way our homes were valued.

List three ways appraisers, agents, or institutions tried to discount your community.

Finish with: Here's what they don't measure, but I do…

Reflection Two

Flipping The Commission Script

Recall a time when outsiders tried to profit off your block's pain, abandoned homes, drug traffic, boarded-up porches.

How was the price set? Who benefited? Who was erased?

Describe how commission-based models promote extraction over restoration.

Write your response: I don't sell struggle, I restore legacy.

Reflection Three

Valuation Through Us, Not At Us

What should an appraiser never assume when walking into a home in your neighborhood?

How do you define value, spiritually, culturally, communally?

What story would you tell about your block if someone gave you a mic for five minutes?

Outline three truths about your property that the system won't ask about, but your legacy demands you document.

Reflection Four

Resisting Their Systems, Writing Our Own

List the "rules" you were taught about homeownership, wealth, and property.

Cross out any that were designed to disqualify, distract, or displace you.

Now rewrite your own rules, five principles you will teach your family, your partners, your successors.

Add one sentence: My home is not their metric, it's our movement.

Reader Activation

This Is Your Blueprint. Now Build It Loud.

If this book spoke your truth...

If you've burned your mortgage, rewritten the rules, or uncovered rhythm under the rubble…

Share your method.

Teach your lesson.

Correct the next system.

Use the included workbook. Host a porch talk. Walk your block like an appraiser would and document what they'll never see without you.

This isn't where the book ends. It's where your legacy begins.

Final Thoughts

You burned the mortgage.

You rewrote the value.

You kept the rhythm.

Now build louder than the blueprint.

Ownership isn't just what you have.

It's how you hold the system accountable.

Legacy moves now, with your name stitched in the foundation.

ABOUT THE AUTHOR

Patrick Dwayne Hall Sr. was born and raised in Inglewood, one of Birmingham, Alabama's most deeply impacted neighborhoods. Surrounded by drug infestation and systemic neglect, he made a quiet promise to himself at age ten: he would flip the strip. Not for profit, but for power. Not to resell it, but to rewrite it.

At 19, Patrick bought his first home. With no formal education in real estate, he educated himself by studying terminology, strategy, and systems, not to become an agent for someone else's company, but to build his own. What he learned was simple and dangerous: someone else had been given the authority to tell him what his property was worth. That truth reshaped his mission forever.

Today, Patrick leads a corporation rooted in education, publishing, investment, mentorship, and personal restoration. He believes that legacy starts with ownership, but only if the owner refuses the outside script. With five children and a vision for generational wealth, he writes, teaches, and builds with one rhythm: set your own value, tell your own story, protect your community, and invest without apology.

His journey is a living blueprint for any reader who feels boxed out of ownership or buried under someone else's definition of worth. If you've never seen success, get around someone who carries it. And if you've ever doubted your ability to change the projector on your family's screen, know this:

Patrick did it. So can you.

OTHER BOOKS PUBLISHED BY P. HALL PUBLISHING AND ENTERTAINMENT LLC

(Available On Amazon & Barnes and noble)

BOUND BY
FLAME
ALARIC FENMOOR

DIAMOND
DOLLS
Stilettos and Steel
ERIC HARRISON SR.

MILLION DOLLAR
TRUCKER
THE SECRET TO A
SUCCESSFUL TRUCKING BUSINESS
RICHARD O CORNELIUS JR.

UNBREAKABLE
TURNING HATERS INTO MOTIVATORS
THE BLACK ALCHEMIST

HEARTS OF
AUBURN
AVENUE
A LOVE STORY
ZORA LARUE

FEDS vs YOU
Sentence Reduction Edition
YOU
PATRICK HALL SR.

BOUND BY
FLAME
PART TWO
ALARIC FENMOOR

DIAMOND
DOLLS II
A Doll Gone Rogue
ERIC HARRISON SR.

THE
700 CLUB
CREDIT CARD
MILLIONAIRE
MALIK WEST

WINGS OF
LEGACY
THE UNTOLD STORY OF
BLACK AVIATION IN AMERICA
FROM ROBBINS, ILLINOIS TO THE STARS
THE RISE
AND FALL OF
FRED HAMPTON
HISTORY YOU SHOULD KNOW

THE
SUPER-
CONSCIOUS
MASTER
THE INNER LAW
THAT CONTROL
POWER, IDENTITY,
AND DESTINY
PATRICK DEWAYNE
HALL SR.

www.ingramcontent.com/pod-product-compliance
Lightning Source LLC
LaVergne TN
LVHW052306200926
848481LV00002B/476
* 9 7 9 8 3 4 9 5 2 2 5 2 9 *